Williams J Rollins

SAN DIEGO TRAVEL GUIDE 2023

Explore Secret Treasures, Stunning Beaches, wildlife & Cuisines with our Ultimate Guide for First-Time Visitors.

Copyright © 2023 by Williams J Rollins

All rights reserved. No part of this publication may be reproduced, stored or transmitted in any form or by any means, electronic, mechanical, photocopying, recording, scanning, or otherwise without written permission from the publisher. It is illegal to copy this book, post it to a website, or distribute it by any other means without permission.

First edition

This book was professionally typeset on Reedsy
Find out more at reedsy.com

Contents

Chapter 1..1

INTRODUCTION TO SAN DIEGO 1

My First time visit to San Diego 1

Historical Background 1

The people 1

Culture 1

San Diego Way of life 1

Chapter 2..12

SAN DIEGO IS CALLING! 12

Weather and Climate 12

Population...12

Currency 12

ATM & Locations 12

Religion 12

Official language 12

Public Holidays..12

Dos & Don't 12

Sacred Architecture 12

Local Custom Law..12

Cultural standards & Restrictions.................................12

Chapter 3..29

ITINERARY BASIC CLUES ENTRY 29

Visa Requirements...29

Who is required to get San Diego visa? 29

Short term visa Application 29

Document needed to apply for San Diego visa 29

How long can a visitor stay with short term visa?.........................29

Chapter 4..35

PLANNING YOUR TRIP...35

Means to get to San Diego..35

Traveling Alone 35

Traveling With children..35

Regions at a Glance 35

Reasons you should visit 35

Best time to visit 35

Packing list 35

Chapter 5..48

GETTING AROUND...48

Air Transportation 48

Land transportation..48

Train Transportation 48

Sea Transportation 48

Transportation Rental Services...48

Chapter 6..53

TIME TO EXPLORE SAN DIEGO..53

Luxury Hotels & prices 53

Beaches to visit...53

Visiting Museums...53

Shopping Malls...53

Nightclubs and Bar 53

Festival & Entertainments 53

Delicious Cuisines 53

Wildlife 53

The Art...53

Flowing waterfalls 53

Jungles to Explore 53

Chapter 7...69

PRIMARY NEEDS IN SAN DIEGO 69

Accommodations options & prices.......................................69

Activities...69

Electric plugs 69

Tour Packages...69

Chapter 8...73

DINING OUT & SHOPPING 73

Dining Out 73

Places to Dine out 73

Places to shop & what to Buy...73

Antiquities Collection...73

Ceramics Collection 73

Coptic Art Collection..73

Textiles Collection..73

Chapter 9...80

HEALTH & SECURITY..80

Health insurance 80

Health Capacity 80

Health-care facilities 80

Security Capacity..80

Security services 80

Chapter 10...88

SURVIVAL GUIDE...88

Tips learn San Diego language 88

Tips to learn San Diego culture 88

Tips to avoid scammers 88

Get used to public transportation.......................................88

Chapter 11...98

HIDDEN GEMS TO DISCOVER 98

Chapter 12..111

FREE MAP APPS FOR LOCATIONS............................111

Chapter 13..116

SOLO TRIP & MEAL PLAN 116

Conclusion 120

1.
   1.
      2.
      3.
      4.
      5.
      6.
2.
   1.
      2.
      3.
      4.
      5.
      6.
      7.

8.

9.

10.

11.

12.

3.

    1.

      2.

      3.

      4.

      5.

      6.

4.

    1.

      2.

      3.

      4.

      5.

      6.

      7.

      8.

5.

    1.

      2.

3.

4.

5.

6.

6.
   1.

   2.

   3.

   4.

   5.

   6.

   7.

   8.

   9.

   10.

   11.

   12.

7.
   1.

   2.

   3.

   4.

   5.

8.

1.
2.
3.
4.
5.
6.
7.
8.
9.
1.
2.
3.
4.
5.
6.
10.
1.
2.
3.
4.
5.
11.
1.
12.
1.

13.

    1.

Chapter 1

INTRODUCTION TO SAN DIEGO

Welcome to San Diego, a world renowned city!

San Diego is a great getaway for all ages, with something for everyone. San Diego is the ideal holiday destination, with its magnificent beaches and spectacular sunsets, as well as its world-class attractions and dynamic culture.

San Diego's beaches provide lots of options for rest and relaxation for anyone searching for a pleasant holiday. Enjoy the stunning vistas from La Jolla Cove or the surf and sunsets from Coronado Beach. Surfing, sailing, kayaking, and other sports are available on the beaches of Mission and Pacific Beach for the more daring.

If you're looking for culture, San Diego has some of the world's most recognized museums. There's something for everyone, from the San Diego Museum of Art to the San Diego Natural History Museum. The iconic San Diego Zoo, Sea World, and Balboa Park are among the other attractions.

San Diego is a foodie's dream when it comes to eating. There's something for everyone with cuisines like Mexican, Italian, and

Asian to select from. San Diego's culinary industry has something for everyone, from world-class restaurants to simple coastal cafés.

San Diego is also a fantastic shopping destination. In addition to its various shopping centers and shops, its many markets provide unusual treasures. Fresh fruit and unusual goods may be found in public markets such as Little Italy Mercato and the Hillcrest Farmers Market.

San Diego offers something for everyone, whether you're searching for a romantic trip or a family holiday. San Diego is the ideal place for your next vacation, with its beautiful beaches, world-class attractions, and dynamic culture.

This travel guide book is intended to give tourists with useful information and tools to help them make the most of their visits to San Diego. It covers a wide range of issues that are critical for a successful and pleasurable travel.

The first advantage of this travel guide book is the vast amount of information it contains. This book includes everything from means of getting to the country to in-depth recommendations on where to go and what to do.

It also contains recommendations on how to save money on lodging, transportation, and food, as well as how to keep safe while traveling.

The book's second advantage is its extensive collection of advice. It provides tips on how to travel securely, save money, and make the most of your vacation.

It also contains information about particular destinations that tourists may like to visit, such as famous attractions, festivals and events, and historical sites.

The book's third advantage is its emphasis on sustainability. It contains suggestions for reducing travel's environmental effect, such as using public transportation and avoiding single-use plastics.

This may assist tourists in making their excursions more environmentally friendly while also lowering their carbon impact.

The fourth advantage is the book's extensive resource list. This book has it everything, from a list of recommended hotels and restaurants, It also provides information on how to get visas and vaccines, as well as tips on staying healthy while traveling.

Lastly, this travel guide book is intended to be an all-inclusive resource for all sorts of tourists.

This book includes the knowledge you need to make the most of your journey, whether you're trekking across the globe, having a family vacation, or simply arranging a weekend escape.

My First time visit to San Diego

One of the most memorable excursions I've ever had was visiting San Diego. When I boarded the aircraft to San Diego, I was filled with excitement and expectation. I'd heard so many good things about this place and couldn't wait to see for myself.

I arrived in San Diego late at night and was instantly taken away by the city's splendor. The skyline lights were so brilliant and welcoming. After checking into my hotel, I decided to go for a stroll about town before retiring for the night. I was enthralled by the majesty of the water as I went down the beach. The sound of the waves smashing on the coast was so calming.

The following day, I decided to see some of San Diego's sites. I went to the San Diego Zoo and was astounded by the variety of creatures I saw. I also got to see some of the beautiful architecture and sculptures in Balboa Park. In that evening, I went for a walk around Seaport Village, where I loved the shopping and restaurants along the shore.

The next day, I planned a day excursion to Coronado Island. I rode a ferry across the bay and got to see some of the city's most spectacular sights. I also got the chance to visit the well-known

Hotel Del Coronado. I couldn't resist taking a plunge in the water since the beach was so beautiful.

On my final day in San Diego, I went on a city tour. From the USS Midway Museum to Sea World, I was able to see all of the key attractions. I was so delighted with all that San Diego has to offer that I departed feeling refreshed and invigorated.

My first trip to San Diego was an unforgettable experience. My vacation exceeded my expectations, from the breathtaking scenery to the unforgettable experiences. I can't wait to return and see more of this amazing city.

It's time for you to tell us about your first visit to San Diego!

Historical Background

San Diego is one of California's oldest cities, with a rich and lively history. When Portuguese explorer Juan Rodriguez Cabrillo landed in what is now San Diego Bay in 1542, it was the first time Europeans saw it. He called the bay San Miguel and the surrounding region San Diego.

The Spaniards erected a fort, or presidio, at San Diego in 1769, and a mission the following year. The presidio and the mission were the earliest European settlements in what is today known as the state of California. The Mission San Diego de Alcala was the first of 21 Spanish missions established in California.

During the Mexican-American War, American soldiers invaded San Diego in 1846. California was accepted as the 31st state to the union two years later. San Diego quickly became a thriving commercial port, with ships arriving from all over the globe.

The railroad revolutionized San Diego in the 1880s, opening up new markets and fostering a thriving tourist sector. San Diego rose to prominence as the "Athens of the West," with an opera theatre, library, and other cultural attractions.

The Panama-California Exposition opened in Balboa Park in 1915, attracting over two million people. San Diego was forever changed by the Exhibition. At this period, the landmark California Tower and the California Building, which today houses the San Diego Museum of Man, were completed.

San Diego's economy moved from a tourism-based to a more diverse one in the 1960s and 1970s, with a concentration on military and high technology. The city underwent a real estate and population boom in the 1980s, and the downtown area was renovated.

San Diego is now a significant metropolis with a population of more than 1.4 million people. It is well-known for its stunning beaches, world-class attractions, and lively culture.

It is still a famous tourist destination and is home to an increasing number of high-tech enterprises.

The people

San Diego is a city in southern California, in the United States. It is the eighth most populous city in the United States and the second most populous city in California, with a population of 1,419,516 as of 2019.

San Diegans are noted for their different origins and interests, and the city attracts a diverse population. People of many races, faiths, nations, and backgrounds make up the city's population. Hispanics (27.6%), non-Hispanic Whites (41.2%), Black Americans (7.6%), Asians (12.8%), and Native Americans (0.7%) are the most prevalent ethnic groupings in San Diego. San Diego also has a sizable immigrant community from Mexico, the Philippines, Vietnam, India, and China.

San Diego embraces education and diversity, and it is home to numerous world-class schools, including the University of California, San Diego, San Diego State University, and the University of San Diego. San Diego also has a diverse range of businesses, from technology and finance to military and aerospace.

San Diegans are renowned for their laid-back lifestyle, and the city offers a variety of outdoor activities and attractions, including beaches, parks, and hiking trails. San Diego is also well-known for its lively nightlife, which includes several restaurants, pubs, and clubs.

The city also has a number of cultural attractions, including the San Diego Zoo and Balboa Park.

San Diego is a city of opportunity, with many entrepreneurs and company owners calling it home. The city is well-known for its robust economy, and it is home to a number of well-known corporations, including Qualcomm, Qualcomm Stadium, and the San Diego Chargers.

San Diego is a city with many distinct cultures and a diverse population. San Diegans are famed for their variety, and the city attracts residents from all walks of life. San Diego is a city that promotes education and diversity, and it is home to a number of world-class institutions.

The city also has a thriving nightlife and is well-known for its many outdoor activities and attractions.

> **San Diego is a city of opportunity, with many entrepreneurs and company owners calling it home.**

Culture

San Diego has a rich cultural and historical heritage. For ages, it has been home to Native American tribes, as well as Spanish settlers and missionaries. The city has experienced a surge in immigration from Mexico and South America, as well as an increase in individuals from other regions of the globe.

The city is recognized for its easygoing, carefree way of life. San Diego's population is varied, with many distinct cultures and customs. The food, art, music, and architecture of the city show the impact of various civilizations.

San Diego boasts a thriving art scene, with several galleries and museums exhibiting works from all ages and countries. The San Diego Museum of Art is the city's biggest art museum, housing pieces from all around the globe. Other art galleries, such as the La Jolla Art Gallery, promote the city's native talent.

Jazz, rock, and mariachi music are all prevalent in the city's music scene. The annual San Diego Music Awards honor the top artists and bands in the city. There are also other live performance venues, such as the Balboa Theater, which feature music events all year.

San Diego also hosts a number of festivals and events that highlight the city's different cultures. The San Diego Cinco de Mayo Festival, which celebrates Mexican culture and tradition, and the San Diego Jewish Film Festival, which presents films from all over the globe, are two examples.

The city is also well-known for its outdoor activities. San Diego features some of the greatest beaches in the world, as well as a diverse variety of recreational opportunities, including hiking, bicycling, surfing, and kayaking. The city also boasts several parks and gardens, which provide an ideal backdrop for outdoor activities.

The culture of San Diego reflects its varied people and colorful past.

The city provides something for everyone, from art and music to festivals and outdoor sports.

San Diego Way of life

The San Diego Way of Life is entirely on enjoying the beautiful outdoors. San Diegans prefer to take advantage of the lovely weather and explore the city's various outdoor attractions, which have an average of 260 sunny days each year.

San Diegans have an active lifestyle, from climbing in the neighboring mountains to surfing in the Pacific Ocean. San Diego is also well-known for its farm-to-table restaurants, artisan breweries, and active nightlife.

> *The city is a melting pot of cultures and customs, making it a dynamic and one-of-a-kind location to live.*

Chapter 2

SAN DIEGO IS CALLING!

San Diego is Calling! one of the most beautiful cities in America, San Diego is the ideal spot to explore and enjoy the great outdoors, with its magnificent beaches, world-class attractions, and limitless outdoor activities.

There's something for everyone here, from the historic Coronado Bridge to the stunning vistas of Balboa Park. So come explore San Diego and create your own wonderful experiences!

Weather and Climate

San Diego, California is a coastal city noted for its pleasant year-round weather and warm temperatures. The city is situated near the Pacific Ocean, which contributes to the city's Mediterranean climate, with warm, dry summers and moderate, rainy winters.

San Diego's typical temperature ranges between 59 and 73 degrees Fahrenheit (15-23 degrees Celsius). Temperatures in the summer vary from the mid-60s to the mid-80s (17-30 degrees Celsius). Temperatures in the winter vary from the mid-50s to the mid-60s (12-18 degrees Celsius). Every year, the city enjoys an average of over 260 sunny days and 11.3 inches (287 millimeters) of rainfall.

The sea wind influences the weather in San Diego. The sea wind helps to keep temperatures temperate during the day and cool at night throughout the summer. The sea wind helps to keep temperatures pleasant throughout the winter.

Because of its diverse geography, San Diego features a number of micro climates. Mountains, coastal locations, lowlands, and desert areas may all be found in the city. As a consequence, various parts of the city experience a broad variety of weather conditions.

San Diego's coastal regions are often warmer and more humid than the city's interior districts. The eastern side of town is colder and drier than the western side. San Diego's mountain and desert parts are more hotter and drier than the coastal sections.

San Diego's summers are often dry and warm. At this time of year, the city usually gets very little rain. June and July are typically the hottest and driest months, with August being the warmest and wettest.

San Diego's winters are often chilly and rainy. At this period, the city normally gets the majority of its rainfall. December and January are often the coldest and wettest months, with February typically being the mildest and driest.

In conclusion The weather and environment of San Diego are fairly pleasant. The city is noted for its pleasant

weather all year, making it a perfect destination to live or visit.

Population

With a population of 1,396,630 as of 2019, San Diego is the seventh biggest city in the United States and the second largest city in California. It is the biggest city in San Diego County, California's most populated county, and the country's second largest county.

San Diego, California's southernmost major city, is situated in a semi-arid, coastal climatic zone. It lies on the Pacific Ocean, just north of the Mexican border. It is home to a big and diversified population from many cultural, ethnic, and economic origins.

San Diego has a greater population density per square mile than the national average of 4,047 persons per square mile. The city has a 59.0% White population, 8.9% African American population, 30.7% Hispanic or Latino population, 8.7% Asian population, and 2.7% Other people. San Diego has a diverse population from all over the globe, including individuals from Europe, Asia, Africa, and Latin America.

San Diego's median age is 34.1 years old, which is somewhat younger than the national norm of 37.5 years old. San Diego's typical household income is $75,453, which is more than the national median of $61,937. San Diego has a poverty rate of 11.5%, which is lower than the national average of 13.1%.

San Diego's population is highly educated, with 42.2% of persons over the age of 25 holding a bachelor's degree or above. San Diego also boasts a sizable military community, with over 30,000 active-duty military people and over 200,000 veterans calling the city home.

San Diego is a rising metropolis that is expected to continue developing in the coming years. By 2023, the population is predicted to reach 1.6 million, and 2 million by 2040.

Currency

San Diego Money is the official currency of the city of San Diego, California. The San Diego County Credit Union issues the money, which is backed by the US dollar.

San Diego Currency is a prepaid debit card that is accepted at all San Diego local and national retailers. The money may be used to purchase products and services both locally and online, making it a handy and safe method of payment.

San Diego currency is available in $5, $10, and $20 amounts. The cards are accepted anywhere Visa and MasterCard are accepted, so they may be used to make transactions in shops, online, and even in other countries. In addition, San Diego Money is accepted at over 1,000 ATM in the San Diego region.

San Diego Currency is issued by the San Diego County Credit Union, which is the sole financial institution in the city. The credit union is a member-owned and run non-profit financial cooperative. The credit union provides a number of services, including savings and bank accounts, loans, credit cards, and San Diego Currencies.

San Diego Currency is a safe and simple method to pay for products and services in the city of San Diego. Unlike cash, San Diego Currency cards are safeguarded by the Visa and MasterCard networks, which means that the money may be quickly restored if the card is lost or stolen. Moreover, the prepaid cards are re loadable, which means that customers may add cash to their card anytime they need to.

Users may save money by eliminating international transaction fees and enjoy the simplicity of making purchases with a single card while using San Diego Currency.

ATM & Locations

1. Bank of America ATM, 1750 East Main Street, El Cajon, California 92021

2. Wells Fargo ATM, located at 8625 Grand Avenue, La Mesa, CA 91942.

3. Chase Bank ATM, La Mesa, CA 91941, 8282 La Mesa Boulevard.

4. 3737 Sports Arena Blvd, San Diego, CA 92110, US Bank ATM

5. ATM Solutions, Oceanside, CA 92054, 2688 Vista Way

6.-Eleven ATM, 1525 Third Avenue, Chula Vista, CA 91911.

7. Wells Fargo ATM, 4161 Genesee Avenue, San Diego, California 92117

8. US Bank ATM, 964 Fifth Avenue, San Diego, CA 92101

9. 7-Eleven ATM, 4025 Bonita Road, Bonita, California 91902

10. Chase Bank ATM, 2901 Jamacha Road, El Cajon, CA 92019.

Religion

San Diego, California has a diverse range of religious beliefs, traditions, and practices. Because of its varied population and closeness to Mexico, the city has become a cultural and religious melting pot.

Christianity is the most prevalent religious tradition in San Diego. This religion is primarily represented by Roman Catholicism, which has been in the city from its inception in 1769.

There are hundreds of Catholic churches in the city, including the historic Mission Basilica San Diego de Alcala, the area's first Catholic mission. Other Christian faiths with a prominent presence in San Diego include Baptists, Methodists, Presbyterians, and Episcopalians.

Judaism is San Diego's second biggest religious tradition. The city has traditionally had a thriving Jewish population, which has expanded dramatically during the last two decades. There are several Jewish synagogues, schools, and other community organizations in the city.

With around 50,000 Muslims, Islam has a substantial presence in San Diego. This demographic is mostly made up of Middle Eastern, African, and South Asian immigrants. A variety of mosques and other Islamic institutions may be found throughout the city.

Other religious traditions practiced in the city include Hinduism, Buddhism, Sikhism, Jainism, and a range of other spiritual practices. San Diego also has an increasing population of atheists, agnostics, and other non-religious people.

In conclusion San Diego is a city of religious tolerance and variety, welcoming and respecting individuals of all faiths. For individuals of various religions, there are several places of worship, community groups, and educational possibilities.

> **San Diego provides something for everyone, whether you want to practice your religion or learn more about another.**

Official language

San Diego, California is home to a varied community of individuals from many origins and cultures. Its variety is mirrored in the city's various official languages. San Diego is the tenth biggest city in the United States, with a population of 1.4 million people, according to the United States Census Bureau.

English is the official language of California and the most widely spoken language in San Diego. According to the most recent United States Census Bureau estimates, more than 59% of San Diegans over the age of five speak solely English at home. With nearly 33% of inhabitants speaking it at home, Spanish is the city's second most widely spoken language.

Tagalog, Vietnamese, Chinese, and Korean are other widely spoken languages.

The City of San Diego acknowledges the significance of delivering services in the language of its citizens and has established a Language Access Program to guarantee that all residents, regardless of language, have access to City services.

Interpretation and translation services are available in over 30 languages, including Spanish, Tagalog, Chinese, Vietnamese, and

Korean. In order to better serve its varied population, the City now offers multilingual services for street signs, papers, websites, and other things.

There are also a number of language-based groups in San Diego that offer educational and cultural services to the city's people. The San Diego Chinese History Society, the Filipino-American Historical Society, the San Diego Vietnamese Association, and the Korean American Association of San Diego are among these groups.

These groups promote cultural understanding and acceptance in the city by offering language lessons, cultural events, and other services to its members.

San Diego is a dynamic and varied city, and the city's numerous official languages reflect that. The Language Access Program of the City of San Diego, as well as the many language-based organizations, work to ensure that all San Diegans have access to the services they need and may communicate in the language that best fits them.

Public Holidays

San Diego celebrates a broad range of official holidays and festivities. From Independence Day through Memorial Day, the city provides several chances for both residents and tourists to celebrate and appreciate the city's culture and customs.

* Independence Day, observed on July 4th, is a well-known celebration in San Diego. The city celebrates with a range of festivities, including parades and concerts as well as customary fireworks displays. The customary reading of the Declaration of Independence on the steps of San Diego City Hall is part of the ceremony.

* The San Diego County Fair, which takes place throughout the summer months of June and July, is one of the city's most popular events. The fair offers a wide range of attractions, cuisine, and entertainment, as well as several exhibits and displays.

* Labor Day is celebrated on the first Monday of September to appreciate the accomplishments of the American worker. The city will commemorate the occasion with a parade and a BBQ.

* Memorial Day is a day set aside to honor those who have served in the military and is generally observed on the final Monday of May. Every year, the city of San Diego organizes a special ceremony to commemorate those who have served at the Veterans Monument in Balboa Park.

* Another major celebration in San Diego is the Fourth of July. The city celebrates with a variety of festivities, including parades and fireworks displays. A customary reading of the Declaration of Independence on the steps of San Diego City Hall is part of the festivities.

* Veterans Day is held on November 11th to honor those who have served in the military. Every year, San Diego holds a unique ceremony at the Veterans Memorial in Balboa Park.

* Christmas Day, which falls on December 25th, is a significant holiday in San Diego. The city has a lot Christmas activities, including caroling and tree lighting ceremonies, as well as parades and concerts.

* New Year's Day, held on January 1st, is a day to celebrate the beginning of a new year. San Diego celebrates with a fireworks show and a parade, among other things.

These are just a handful of the numerous public holidays and festivals that San Diego observes. There are other more events, such as Cinco de Mayo, the San Diego LGBT Parade, and the San Diego Marathon.

> **There are lots of ways to celebrate in San Diego, whether you're a native or a guest.**

Dos & Don't

Do's

• Go to the beaches such as La Jolla Shores, Ocean Beach, Coronado Beach, and Mission Beach.

• Pay a visit to the San Diego Zoo and its Safari Park.

• Go to Balboa Park, which has numerous museums, parks, and attractions, and take a harbor boat or a whale-watching trip.

• Dine at one of the many coastal restaurants in La Jolla or the Gas lamp District.

• Visit the various neighborhoods and their local cuisine.

• Have a good time in the nightlife in the Gas lamp District or Pacific Beach.

Don'ts

• While visiting the beaches, remember to bring a hat and sunglasses.

• Bring a wet suit if you want to participate in aquatic sports.

• Don't forget to bring sunscreen and a towel for sun protection.

• Before entering the sea, be sure to check the tide charts.

• If the waves are too high, avoid swimming in the water.

• Never leave your valuables unattended in public.

• Do not park your automobile on the street overnight.

Sacred Architecture

San Diego is home to many beautiful, unique, and sacred architectural structures, ranging from the Mission Basilica San Diego de Alcalá—the first of Father Junipero Serra's chain of 21 California missions—to the historic Balboa Park, which hosted the 1935 California Pacific International Exposition and the San Diego Zoo.

Other notable spiritual constructions in the neighborhood include the Chicano Park mural in Barrio Logan, the renowned St. James Cathedral, and the Cathedral of Our Lady of the Rosary, among many more churches and religious buildings.

These buildings reflect San Diego's rich history and culture, with many of them dating back hundreds of years.

> **San Diego's sacred architecture reflects both its indigenous and Spanish-colonial heritage, and many of its monuments are notable landmarks that are visited and loved by both residents and visitors.**

Local Custom Law

San Diego's local custom law is complicated and diverse. It consists of various state, county, and municipal legislation, as well as judicial judgments. This sort of legislation oversees connections in the city between persons and companies, as well as between the city and its citizens and the city and the state.

Local custom rules are intended to safeguard individuals' and companies' rights while also ensuring the city's order and stability. They are also meant to encourage economic development and prosperity.

Local custom laws are based on the California Civil Code, which serves as the state's legal framework. The California Civil Code is split into many parts, each with its own set of laws and regulations. There are a number of particular statutes connected to local custom law in San Diego included in the California Civil Code.

Zoning rules, building codes, business regulations, health and safety requirements, and environmental controls are all examples of local custom laws. All of these regulations exist to safeguard the public from possible damage and to preserve the city's and its people' safety.

Local custom rules also control the buying and sale of real estate, as well as the transfer of property rights. These laws are often referred to as property law in San Diego. Property law is meant to safeguard both property owners' and purchasers' and sellers' rights.

Laws governing the issuing of licenses, permits, and registrations are examples of local custom laws. These laws are intended to guarantee that companies in the city follow the law and deliver services that meet the standards established by the state and municipal.

Local custom laws control residents' rights to engage in different types of public service, including as voting and jury duty. These laws are meant to guarantee that people' rights are exercised in a fair and equal way.

San Diego custom law is complicated and ever-changing. It is critical that citizens and companies understand the laws that apply to them in order to preserve their rights and interests.

> **As a result, while dealing with local custom law in San Diego, it is always best to speak with an experienced attorney.**

Cultural standards & Restrictions

San Diego is recognized for its broad cultural history, although certain cultural prohibitions and norms still exist. These cultural norms and constraints are vital to the San Diego community because they serve to keep the culture alive and well.

The clothing code is the most visible cultural norm in San Diego. Several forms of clothes are thought to be unsuitable or offensive. This includes any exposing apparel or anything with inappropriate words or pictures written on it. Also, it is critical to dress correctly for the weather and the event.

The language used in San Diego is another cultural norm. While English is the predominant language spoken in San Diego, other languages are spoken in specific regions of the city. Other languages spoken in specific areas of the city include Spanish, Vietnamese, and Tagalog.

San Diego also has a rigorous anti-drug and alcohol policy. Drinking and narcotics are not permitted in public areas and are severely prohibited. Before going out, it is essential to understand the regulations concerning alcohol and drugs.

San Diego has strong restrictions governing public conduct as well. This includes public drunkenness, disruptive behavior, and trash. It is essential to be courteous to others in public and to observe all applicable rules and regulations.

Lastly, San Diego is proud of its cultural legacy. This includes things like observing traditional festivals, following local traditions, learning the local language and culture, and caring for the environment. Before visiting the location, it is essential to grasp the local culture and traditions.

San Diego has high cultural norms and regulations in place. These rules and regulations are necessary to preserve San Diego's culture, to keep the local culture alive and healthy, and to guarantee that everyone in the community is respected.

While visiting San Diego, it is essential to follow certain guidelines and regulations.

Chapter 3

ITINERARY BASIC CLUES ENTRY

Traveling has become a popular hobby for many people all over the globe, which necessitates the need for knowledge and direction to help organize a memorable trip. A travel guide may help you choose the appropriate place, organize an itinerary, and make the most of your vacation.

An itinerary is a precise schedule of your whole journey, from the time you depart to the time you arrive at your destination. It may contain all of the locations you want to go, activities you want to do, and the amount of time you want to spend at each destination.

This travel guide book will provide you all the information you need to plan your trip, including itinerary essentials like entrance requirements, visas, and currency exchange rates. This is an outline of itinerary fundamentals to consider while organizing your vacation.

Visa Requirements

The duration of stay in San Diego is determined by the traveler's nationality, purpose of visit, and length of stay. Visitors from certain nations may, in general, be needed to get a visa before going to the United States.

Who is required to get San Diego visa?

The San Diego visa is a kind of visa provided by the US Department of State to residents and nationals of specified countries who want to visit the US but are not eligible for a normal visa.

To be eligible for a San Diego visa, the applicant must satisfy specific requirements. They must have a valid passport from their home country, be visiting the US for a specified reason such as business, study, tourism, or family visit, and have the finances to sustain themselves throughout their stay. Candidates must also have no history of visa overstays or other immigration offenses, as well as a clean criminal background.

Moreover, candidates must establish strong links to their home country that will motivate them to return following their stay to the

United States. This might include proof of a family in their native country, a job they want to return to, or a company they own.

Applicants may also be needed to produce proof of financial resources, such as bank statements or other proof that they have enough money to meet their costs while in the United States. They may also be required to present documentation such as an invitation letter from a US citizen or a copy of their trip schedule.

Candidates must appear in person for an interview at their home country's US consulate or embassy. They will be asked questions about their reason for visiting the United States and their plans while they are here during the interview.

Anybody who wants to visit San Diego and satisfies the following requirements may be eligible to apply for a San Diego visa.

Short term visa Application

It might be difficult to apply for a short-term visa to San Diego. To have the highest chance of success, it is essential to complete all of the stages and submit all of the needed documentation.

Initially, you must determine the sort of visa you are seeking for. Tourist visas, business visas, student visas, and other visas are all available for short-term visits in San Diego. The kind of visa you pick will be determined by the purpose of your stay, so you must know what you want to accomplish in San Diego before making your choice.

After deciding on the sort of visa you want, you must complete the relevant paperwork and send them to the consulate or embassy. Provide copies of your passport and any other papers that may be necessary (such as proof of financial stability, or proof of your ties to your home country).

You must wait for a response from the consulate after submitting your visa application. This procedure may take anything from two weeks to many months, depending on the kind of visa you apply for and the complexity of your application.

After your visa application is granted, you will be given a visa number and information on how to receive your visa. Often, this entails paying a fee and making an appointment with the consulate or embassy.

You must submit your visa and passport at the border when you arrive in San Diego. Before you may enter the nation, you must first pass through a series of inspections and interviews.

It's vital to keep in mind that a short-term visa does not ensure you'll be able to remain in San Diego for the length of your vacation. You must follow all of the rules and regulations in effect in the United States, and any infractions may result in deportation or other legal action.

Applying for a short-term visa to San Diego may be a hard procedure, but following these steps will help assure the success of your application. Best wishes!

Document needed to apply for San Diego visa

A person must produce the following papers when applying for a visa to go to San Diego, California:

1. A valid passport with at least six months validity left.

2. A completed DS-160 Non immigrant Visa Application Form

3. A passport-sized picture taken in the last six months

4. Evidence of adequate financial means to cover the length of the vacation

5. Evidence of hotel or alternative lodging arrangements in San Diego

6. A valid itinerary for travel and/or a round-trip ticket

7. Any relevant supporting papers, such as evidence of work, a letter of invitation from a San Diego host, or documentation to verify the purpose of the visit.

How long can a visitor stay with short term visa?

It is determined on the sort of visa the traveler possesses. Visitors on a B-1/B-2 visa are generally permitted to remain in the United States for up to six months.

It is crucial to remember, however, that the US Customs and Border Protection (C.B.P) has the authority to restrict a visitor's stay to fewer than 6 months.

Chapter 4

PLANNING YOUR TRIP

Step 1: Determine When You Wish to Go

San Diego is a famous tourist destination due to its pleasant weather all year. Summer is the most popular season, with temperatures ranging from the mid-70s to the mid-80s with occasional heat waves.

With temperate temperatures, spring and autumn are also wonderful seasons to visit. With temperatures in the 60s and occasional rain, winter is the least favored season. Determine when you want to travel and check the weather prediction before you depart.

Step 2: Reserve Your Flight

Plan a flight to San Diego International Airport (SAN), the area's major airport. If you're flying in from a smaller airport, you may need to change planes. To obtain the cheapest pricing, do your homework and buy your tickets well in advance.

Step 3: Determine Your Accommodations

San Diego offers a wide range of hotels, from low-cost motels to luxury resorts. Choose the style of lodging you want and look for the greatest offers. To get the greatest value for your money, read reviews and compare rates before making a reservation.

Step 4: Arrange Your Activities

San Diego offers a wide range of activities and attractions to enjoy. There's something for everyone, from the touristic attractions of Sea World and the San Diego Zoo to the stunning beaches and the historic Gas lamp Quarter. Arrange your activities ahead of time to avoid missing out on anything.

Step 5: Schedule Your Transportation

San Diego has an excellent public transit system, but if you want to explore the city more freely, you should hire a vehicle. To obtain the best bargain, compare costs and book your transportation in advance.

Step 6: Pack Your Luggage

Pack everything you'll need for your vacation, including comfy shoes, sunscreen, and a camera. Depending on the time of year, you may wish to bring a light jacket or sweater for the chilly nights.

"More details on packing list will be revealed in this chapter no panic!"

Step 7: Have a good time!

It's time to unwind and enjoy your vacation in San Diego now that you've arrived.

Tour the city, try different eateries, and take plenty of photographs. Have a good time and make the most of your vacation!

Means to get to San Diego

San Diego, California, is a lovely seaside city in the state's south. It is a popular tourist and local destination due to its sunny environment, prominent attractions, and dynamic culture. Depending on your budget and chosen method of transportation, there are many ways to travel to San Diego.

If you want to go to San Diego as quickly as possible, flying is the best option. The principal airport in the region is San Diego International Airport (SAN), which provides direct flights from many major cities across the globe. You may also fly into Mexico's Tijuana International Airport (TIJ) and take a bus to San Diego.

Driving is an excellent way to save money if you want to save money. San Diego is just a few hours' drive from Los Angeles, and multiple interstates and roads link the two cities. The route is beautiful, and there are several spots to stop along the way.

If you want to take a more adventurous route to San Diego, you may take the train. Amtrak operates multiple routes connecting San Diego to large cities such as Los Angeles, San Francisco, and Seattle. The train is an excellent way to experience the California countryside, and you may even take an overnight train if desired.

You may also get to San Diego via bus. Greyhound and Mega bus both provide trips to San Diego from a variety of places in the United States and Canada. The buses are inexpensive and dependable, and they can bring you to San Diego in a matter of hours.

Lastly, you may get to San Diego via boat. San Diego lies on the Pacific Coast and has a number of ports of call. You may take a cruise ship from Los Angeles or San Francisco to San Diego in a matter of days.

You'll have a fantastic time regardless of how you travel to San Diego!

Traveling Alone

Going to San Diego alone may be a fantastic experience, particularly if you want to see one of the most beautiful cities in the United States. San Diego is well-known for its pleasant weather, beautiful beaches, and exciting attractions.

San Diego provides something for everyone, whether you want a quiet holiday or an action-packed vacation. Here are some suggestions for making the most of your solo vacation to San Diego.

Plan your itinerary beforehand. San Diego has a lot to offer, and it might be difficult to cram everything into a short vacation. Be sure you investigate the city and pick which attractions are must-sees and which may be skipped.

To save money, consider staying in one of the city's numerous hotels or hostels, or perhaps renting a room in a shared apartment.

Second, keep safety in mind. While San Diego is typically a safe place, it's always a good idea to remain mindful of your surroundings when traveling alone.

Be in well-lit and busy locations, be alert of your surroundings, and follow your instincts if you ever feel uneasy. Also, keep your valuables close to hand and be cautious with your sensitive information.

Make the most of the city's attractions. From the world-famous San Diego Zoo to the USS Midway Museum, San Diego has numerous great attractions. Outdoor activities such as surfing, kayaking, and biking are also available. Don't forget to see the city's stunning beaches.

Lastly, don't be frightened to interact with new individuals. San Diego is a terrific area to meet new people, so don't be hesitant to strike up a conversation with a local or participate in group activities. You might also join a meeting group or a walking tour to learn more about the city.

Going to San Diego by yourself may be a fantastic experience. You can make the most of your vacation with a little forethought and caution. Just remember to do your homework, be safe, enjoy the city's attractions, and don't be scared to meet new people.

You may enjoy the finest solo vacation ever if you follow these suggestions.

(More details on Solo trip)
(chapter 13)

Traveling With children

Visiting San Diego with children may be a fantastic experience. San Diego is an excellent location for children of all ages, since it provides a wide range of attractions and activities. There are several locations to explore and enjoy, ranging from the world-renowned San Diego Zoo and Sea World San Diego to Lego land California.

There are a few important factors to consider while planning a vacation to San Diego with children. Then, choose lodgings that will meet the requirements of your family. San Diego offers a diverse selection of hotels, resorts, and vacation rentals, as well as campsites and RV parks. You should also organize your schedule so that you have enough time to visit the city's main attractions.

San Diego provides something for everyone in terms of activities. Try heading to the beach, taking a harbor tour, or exploring Balboa Park. Consider bringing the kids to Sea World or Lego land for an added dose of entertainment. If you want something more low-key, you might visit the city's various museums and cultural sites.

There are several possibilities for places to dine with children in San Diego. Restaurants in San Diego range from family-friendly quick food joints to elegant dining venues. There are also several food trucks and street sellers around town, serving a wide range of economical and excellent dishes.

When it comes to moving about in San Diego, public transit is a cost-effective choice. San Diego's Metropolitan Transportation System (MTS) operates bus, trolley, and light rail systems across the city. There are also several taxi and ride-sharing services, as well as bike-share programs, accessible.

And most importantly make sure you're prepared in case of an emergency. In case of an emergency, make sure you have a first-aid kit, sunscreen, and a list of emergency contacts.

San Diego is an excellent choice for families wishing to explore the city and have a good time.

With so many sights and activities to choose from, you're sure to find something for everyone in your family.

Regions at a Glance

San Diego is the second-largest city in California and the eighth-largest in the United States, situated in the southwestern United States. San Diego, with a population of over 1.3 million people, is recognized as "America's Finest City" because of its moderate temperature, magnificent beaches, and distinct culture.

Downtown San Diego is the city's commercial and cultural hub, with a thriving nightlife, multiple museums, and the historic Gas lamp Quarter. With 1,200 acres of gardens, paths, and attractions, Balboa Park is the biggest urban park in the United States. It is also the location of the world-famous San Diego Zoo.

Several of San Diego's most popular beaches are located in North County, including La Jolla, Encinitas, and Carlsbad. The area is well-known for its relaxed lifestyle and breathtaking beach vistas.

Several of San Diego's most popular attractions, such as Mission Trails Regional Park and San Diego's Wild Animal Park, are located in East County. The region is also well-known for its beautiful mountain scenery and outdoor sports.

The South Bay is San Diego's entry point to Mexico. Tijuana, Mexico's border town, and the famous beaches of Imperial Beach and Coronado are located in the area.

Central San Diego is a diversified neighborhood that includes the city's historic districts such as Old Town, Hill crest, and North Park. The Museum of Man and Balboa Park are among the cultural attractions in the neighborhood.

San Diego offers something for everyone, whether you're searching for a quiet day at the beach, an adventure in the great outdoors, or a cultural experience.

San Diego, with its broad assortment of activities, is an excellent location for exploring and experiencing the finest of California.

Reasons you should visit

San Diego has plenty to offer everyone. San Diego offers it everything, whether you want a calm beach holiday, exhilarating outdoor activities, or a dynamic city life experience. These are some of the top reasons to visit San Diego.

1. **The Weather**: San Diego is recognized for its year-round bright sky and temperate temps. Even in the winter, temperatures seldom fall below 60 degrees Fahrenheit. This makes it suitable for outdoor activities such as hiking, kayaking, riding, and other outdoor sports.

2. **The Beaches**: San Diego is home to some of the world's greatest beaches. San Diego offers a beach for everyone, whether you want a quiet day on the sand or an adrenaline-pumping excursion. La Jolla, Mission Beach, Pacific Beach, and Coronado are all popular destinations.

3. **Outdoor Activities:** San Diego has a plethora of outdoor activities for people of all ages. There is something for everyone, from hiking and bicycling at Torrey Pines State Park to surfing in Ocean Beach.

4. **The Food Scene**: San Diego is well-known for its diversified and tasty culinary culture. There is something for every taste and budget, from mom-and-pop restaurants to expensive diners.

5. **The Culture**: San Diego has a thriving and diversified culture. There's lots to see and do in San Diego, from the busy Gas lamp Quarter to the museums and galleries of Balboa Park.

6. **Shopping:** San Diego is a shopper's dream. There is something for everyone, from world-class shopping centers to farmers markets.

7. **The Nightlife**: San Diego has a vibrant nighttime scene. There is something for everyone, whether you want a calm evening out or a crazy night on the town.

> **So, what are you holding out for? Pack your luggage and prepare to discover all San Diego has to offer.**

This magnificent city has something for everyone with its fantastic weather, beaches, outdoor activities, culinary scene, culture, shopping, and nightlife.

Best time to visit

San Diego is a renowned tourist destination in the United States. It is well-known for its pleasant temperature and plethora of attractions. The city is situated on California's Pacific Coast, near the Mexican border. San Diego is a terrific city to visit all year because of its magnificent beaches, world-class attractions, and dynamic culture.

So, what is the greatest time of year to visit San Diego?

In general, the ideal months to visit San Diego are from March to May and September to November. This is when the weather is nice and the crowds are few. Throughout these months, there will be lots of sunlight and pleasant temperatures, making it ideal for spending time outside.

Temperatures may be extremely high during the summer months of June through August, and the city is generally quite congested. Summer is a terrific time to come if you can take the heat and congestion, since there are lots of outdoor things to do, such as swimming, surfing, and boating.

If you prefer a more leisurely vacation, try visiting San Diego during the winter months of December through February. Even if the temperatures are lower and the people are less, there is still much to do and see. You may also take advantage of the many holiday activities and celebrations that occur during this time.

Whichever time of year you visit San Diego, there will be plenty of attractions, activities, and events to keep you amused.

San Diego provides something for everyone, whether you want a quiet beach vacation, an action-packed adventure, or a cultural experience.

Packing list

- **Hats**
  - **First-aid kit.**
  - **Comfy walking shoes**
  - **Lightweight jacket**
  - **Sunscreen**
  - **Sunglasses**
  - **Swimwear**
  - **Beach towel**
  - **Camera**
  - **Portable charger**
  - **A portable water bottle**
  - **Snacks**
  - **Maps/GPS**
  - **Toiletries**

Chapter 5

GETTING AROUND

San Diego is a busy and interesting city to visit, with several transportation options. The Metropolitan Transportation System (MTS) provides access to buses, trolleys, and Coaster trains, making public transit the most popular and convenient mode of commuting.

San Diego International Airport, which offers various domestic and international flights, is also a popular choice for vacationers.

San Diego has an enormous motorway system as well as lots of parking for people who want to drive. Visitors may also explore the city on foot or by bike, taking use of the many bike routes and trails.

Air Transportation

Southwest, American Airlines, Delta, and United are among the carriers that provide domestic flights inside San Diego. Flight prices vary depending on the airline, route, and time of year, but they often range from **$30 to $200**.

There are also a number of helicopter services available for travel in and around San Diego. Depending on the distance and length of the flight, these services might range from **$50 to $500** per person.

Land transportation

To travel about San Diego, there are many modes of transportation accessible.

1. **Public Transportation**: The San Diego Metropolitan Transit System (MTS) operates buses, trolleys, and the Coaster train across the city of San Diego. A one-way ticket costs **$2.50.**

2. **Ride-Hailing**: Uber and Lyft are prominent ride-hailing services in San Diego. Costs vary based on the service chosen, but range from **$4 to $15** depending on distance and time of day.

3. **Taxis:** Taxis are readily accessible in San Diego. Costs per mile generally vary from **$3.50 to $6.50.**

4. **Bicycle:** Bicycles are an excellent mode of transportation in San Diego. Bicycles may be hired for **$1 every 30 minutes** through bike-share firms such as Ofo and Lime.

5. Walking is a terrific method to get about and it is free! Yeah it's absolutely Free everywhere

Train Transportation

San Diego has three public transit systems that serve the whole city.

• **San Diego Metropolitan** Transportation System (MTS) - MTS provides bus, trolley, and Rapid bus services across San Diego for **$2.50 one-way.**

• **North County Transit District** :(NCTD) - NCTD provides bus and train services in the North County region for **$2.50 one-way.**

• **San Diego Coaster** : The San Diego Coaster is a commuter train line that travels from Oceanside to downtown San Diego for **$5.00 one-way.**

Sea Transportation

The ferry is the most frequent means to get about San Diego via water. The San Diego Bay Ferry, operated by the San Diego Harbor Excursion, runs between Broadway Pier and the Coronado Ferry Landing. It also provides a harbor tour and whale viewing trips.

Water taxis, kayaks, paddle boards, jet skis, and sailboats are some of the additional water transportation alternatives in San Diego. Water transportation services are provided by a number of boat rental firms and charter services in the region. There are also a number of tour companies that provide boat excursions of San Diego Bay.

Prices are also fair. The San Diego Bay Ferry, for example, **sells a one-way ticket for $4.50.**

> **Visit the San Diego Harbor Excursion website for additional information about boat transportation in San Diego.**

Transportation Rental Services

San Diego transportation rental options make it easy to navigate about the city. There are several transportation rental businesses to select from, whether you need a short journey to the airport or a leisurely ride through town.

Taxis, ride-sharing services, and automobile rental services are the most common modes of transportation in San Diego. Taxis are the most convenient mode of transportation in town since they are accessible at all major airports, hotels, and tourist destinations.

These are usually the most costly choice, with costs ranging between **$2 and $4 per mile**. Ride-sharing services like Uber and Lyft are becoming more popular in San Diego and provide a more cost-effective way to move about town.

Ride-sharing services normally charge between **$1 and $2 per mile.** When it comes to mobility throughout San Diego, car rental companies like Enterprise, Avis, and Hertz provide the greatest options. Costs range from $20 to $50 a day, depending on the type and model of the vehicle.

Whichever form of transportation rental service you choose, it is important to review the company's fees and policies before committing to a service.

Several firms have a minimum fee or time restriction, so check the small print before scheduling a journey. It is also critical to ensure that the firm you hire is reliable and has a strong safety record.

San Diego transportation rental services provide a simple and economical method to move about the city.

There are several alternatives available, whether you want a short journey to the airport or a more leisurely excursion through town.

Chapter 6

TIME TO EXPLORE SAN DIEGO

Experiencing San Diego is unlike any other experience. There is something to explore around every turn, from its spectacular natural beauty to its lively culture and different communities. San Diego offers something for everyone, whether you choose to explore the city's outdoor attractions, enjoy the local art and food, or just relax on the beach.

The city has some of the most beautiful beaches in the United States, with miles of sand and surf for everyone to enjoy. Coronado Beach is a popular swimming, surfing, and sunbathing destination, while La Jolla Cove is a picturesque site to take in the coastline's spectacular vistas.

Nature enthusiasts will enjoy Torrey Pines State Natural Reserve, which is home to some of the world's most unusual and endangered flora.

The Gas lamp District is the place to go for those seeking more urban action. This vibrant neighborhood is densely packed with restaurants, bars, and stores, as well as several entertainment alternatives. Balboa Park, with its beautiful gardens, historic landmarks, and world-class art galleries, is also a terrific place to spend a day exploring.

Whatever you choose to do with your stay in San Diego, you will have an amazing experience. So pack your luggage and prepare for an adventure unlike any other.

Luxury Hotels & prices

The Fairmont Grand Del Mar, which costs $399 per night.

The US Grant, a Luxury Collection Hotel, costs $259 per night.

Hotel Del Coronado (379 dollars per night)

The Westgate Hotel costs $199 per night.

Kimpton Palomar Hotel in San Diego - $229 per night

The Sofia Hotel costs $199 per night.

Hotel La Valencia - $299 per night

The Hard Rock Hotel in San Diego costs $229 per night.

Omni Hotel in San Diego - $219 per night

The Bristol Hotel costs $179 per night.

Beaches to visit

1. **Coronado Beach -** This beautiful beach has been dubbed one of the greatest in the United States. It's ideal for first-time visitors, thanks to its gorgeous white sand, tranquil waves, and spectacular vistas.

2. **La Jolla Shores -** With its shallow seas and sandy shoreline, this beach is great for families. La Jolla Shores is also home to the famed La Jolla Cove, where you can go kayaking, snorkeling, and participate in other water activities.

3. **Mission Beach -** Mission Beach's two-mile boardwalk is ideal for rollerblading, bicycling, and people-watching. Belmont Park, an amusement park featuring a classic wooden roller coaster, is also located on this shore.

4. **Pacific Beach -** This beach is well-known for its excellent surfing and sunbathing opportunities. It's also well-known for its nightlife, having a plethora of pubs and restaurants to choose from.

5. **Ocean Beach -** For those looking to explore the San Diego coastline, this beach is ideal. It's a terrific place for a first-time tourist, with its pier, surf shops, cafés, and other attractions.

Visiting Museums

San Diego Air and Space Museum: Situated in historic Balboa Park, this museum provides an overview of aviation, space exploration, and other topics.

USS Midway Museum: Situated at Navy Pier in downtown San Diego, this museum provides an overview of the US Navy's history, including a visit of the aircraft carrier USS Midway.

Old Town San Diego State Historic Park: Situated in Old Town San Diego, this park provides an overview of California and San Diego history from the days of the Spanish Empire to the advent of the US Navy in San Diego.

San Diego Natural History Museum: Situated in Balboa Park, this museum provides an overview of the region's natural history, including animals, plants, and geology.

Maritime Museum of San Diego: Situated in downtown San Diego, this museum provides an overview of the area's nautical history, including a visit of the Star of India, the world's oldest operating sailing vessel.

Museum of Photographic Arts: Situated in Balboa Park, this museum examines the history of photography via both historic and contemporary works.

San Diego Museum of Man: Situated in Balboa Park, this museum examines human history from ancient civilizations to present societies.

San Diego Museum of Art: Situated in Balboa Park, this museum explores the history of art via classic and contemporary pieces.

Shopping Malls

*Mission Valley Westfield

*Westfield Technical College

*Fashion Valley Shopping Center

*Otay Ranch Town Center

*Seaport Village

*Premium Outlets Las Americas

*Parkway Plaza

*Viejas Outlet Center

*Carlsbad Premium Outlets

*Las Posas Plaza Shopping Center

Nightclubs and Bar

1. **The Tipsy Crow:** This renowned Gaslamp Quarter pub serves creative drinks, a large range of beers, and a dance floor for late-night merriment.

2. **The Ould Sod Irish Pub & Restaurant:** This Normal Heights neighborhood bar has a comfortable environment, live music, and classic Irish pub cuisine like bangers and mash.

3. **The Brew Project:** This Mission Hills craft beer pub serves house-made beer, a changing variety of craft cans and bottles, and a menu of upscale bar foods.

4. **The Pearl Hotel:** This Point Loma retro-chic hotel has an outdoor pool, live music, and a tiki-inspired poolside bar.

5. **The Aerobar:** This oceanfront bar in Pacific Beach offers artisan drinks, panoramic ocean views, pool tables, and dart boards.

6. **Analog Bar:** This East Village hipster dive pub offers a changing assortment of specialty beers, live DJs, and an outside terrace.

7. **The Nolen:** This East Village rooftop bar above The Nolen offers handmade drinks, panoramic city views, and live DJs and music.

8. **Bar Dynamite:** This Hillcrest dive pub has a friendly environment, inexpensive drinks, and a jukebox with a selection of music.

9. **The Rail:** An upmarket Gaslamp Quarter pub serves specialty drinks, live music, and a small nibbles menu.

10. **The Sandbar Sports Grill:** This Pacific Beach seaside bar has over 50 Televisions, a large range of beer and drinks, and a menu of pub cuisine.

Festival & Entertainments

1. **San Diego County Fair:** The San Diego County Fair, held every summer at the Del Mar Fairgrounds, is one of the county's finest events. The fair is a terrific way to get your San Diego entertainment fix, with fair rides, deep-fried snacks, live music, animal exhibitions, and lots of carnival games.

2. **SeaWorld San Diego:** For first-time visitors, this aquatic theme park is a must-see. Come up up and personal with whales, dolphins, sea lions, and other water creatures. In addition, there are exhilarating coasters, a water park, and lots of entertainment options.

3. **Balboa Park:** Its 1,200-acre urban park has 15 important museums, several parks and open spaces, and the world-renowned San Diego Zoo. There are also several theaters, galleries, and other entertainment venues located throughout the park.

4. **The Old Town San Diego State Historic Park:** Go back in time and discover this re-creation of San Diego's Mexican and early American era. Old Town is a terrific place to see early San Diego, with colorful architecture, small shops, and lots of entertainment.

5. **Gaslamp Quarter:** The Gaslamp Quarter is a 16-block area in downtown San Diego. It's the ideal area to sample some of the city's nightlife, with a plethora of restaurants, pubs, and nightclubs.

6. **San Diego Beaches:** San Diego has miles of coastline and is ideal for beachgoers. There's a beach for everyone, whether you want to soak up some rays, catch a wave, or just enjoy the landscape.

7. **La Jolla Cove**: Both residents and visitors go to La Jolla Cove. La Jolla Cove is a terrific site to enjoy San Diego's natural beauty, with its little beach, tidal pools, and sea caves.

8. **San Diego Zoo:** The San Diego Zoo is one of the top zoos in the world, with over 4,000 species. The zoo is home to several different animals, such as pandas, elephants, and koalas.

9. **San Diego Symphony:** The San Diego Symphony is one of the oldest orchestras in America. The symphony presents an outstanding range of musical performances, from classical to modern.

10. **Coronado Island:** This little island is ideal for getting away from the hustle and bustle of downtown San Diego. Coronado Island, with its beaches, restaurants, and stores, is a terrific spot to unwind and take in the landscape.

Delicious Cuisines

1. **Mexican:** San Diego is well-known for its Mexican cuisine, and with cause. Tacos al pastor, carne asada, and enchiladas are popular traditional foods.

2. **Seafood:** San Diego is famous for its fresh seafood, so try fish tacos, ceviche, and clam chowder.

3. **Barbecue:** San Diego has some of the greatest barbecue in the state. Slow-cooked ribs, smoked brisket, and pulled pork are all good options.

4. **Asian Fusion:** San Diego is home to some of the country's top Asian fusion eateries. Korean-Mexican tacos, ramen burgers, and sushi burritos are all options.

5. **Craft Beer:** San Diego is known as the craft beer center of the United States, so try some of the local beers. Local brewers provide IPAs, sours, and stouts.

Wildlife

San Diego is an excellent first-time tourist location for exploring the city's plentiful wildlife. The city has a diverse range of environments, from coastal lagoons and estuary to mountains and deserts, making it a home for a wide range of animal species.

Whether you want to see migrating birds, watch whales, or learn about the region's numerous local species, San Diego offers something for everyone.

The San Diego Zoo Safari Park is an excellent spot to begin your animal excursion. The Safari Park, located just outside of Escondido, is home to a diverse range of animals from all over the globe. You may see and interact with African animals such as rhinos, lions, zebras, and giraffes, as well as other continents' fauna such as kangaroos and koalas.

The park also features a vast aviary full of colorful birds and shelters numerous endangered species such as the California condor and the Hawaiian goose. There are additional educational activities available in the park, such as an animal encounter program, guided safaris, and even a "Ride the Wild" excursion.

La Jolla Cove is the place to go if you want to get up close and personal with wildlife. There is a diverse range of aquatic life here, including leopard sharks, sea lions, and even the rare sea turtle. The sheltered waters make it an excellent location for snorkeling and scuba diving, and you'll get a terrific view of the seals and sea lions sunning on the rocks.

Moreover, La Jolla Cove is a favorite whale-watching location, particularly during the winter months when gray whales travel through the region.

Visit the Cleveland National Forest for a more rustic animal encounter. There are a number of ecosystems can be found here, including oak woods, chaparral, and wetlands. Wildlife found in the forest includes black bears, coyotes, bobcats, and mountain lions.

In addition, the forest is an excellent place to go bird watching, since it is home to a wide variety of raptors, songbirds, and ducks. In addition to hiking paths, the Cleveland National Forest has camping and picnic spots.

Don't forget to visit the San Diego Bay National Wildlife Refuge. This sanctuary is home to a wide range of birds, including herons, pelicans, and terns, as well as endangered species such as the California least tern and the brown pelican.

The refuge is also a haven for natural animals such as fish, turtles, and crabs. There are additional educational events available in the refuge, such as guided boat cruises, bird-watching tours, and lectures.

San Diego is an excellent choice for a first-time tourist wishing to discover the city's diverse fauna. There are several animal watching possibilities across the city, ranging from the San Diego Zoo Safari Park to the Cleveland National Forest.

So grab your binoculars and prepare to explore San Diego's wild side!

The Art

San Diego is a thriving coastal city in Southern California. It is well-known for its beautiful beaches, pleasant climate, and relaxed way of life, but it is also a cultural hub with a booming art scene.

From its various museums and galleries to its one-of-a-kind public art pieces, the city provides a diverse range of art experiences. At

Balboa Park, the San Diego Museum of Art has an extraordinary collection of paintings from all around the globe and throughout history.

The Museum of Contemporary Art San Diego exhibits works by established as well as rising contemporary artists. The Timken Museum of Art and the San Diego Art Institute are two more significant institutions.

Annual art events in San Diego include the San Diego Festival of the Arts and the San Diego Comic-Con International. The San Diego Public Art Program commissions and maintains hundreds of public art works around the city, ranging from park sculptures to murals and mosaics in public locations.

The city also has a vibrant music culture, with various venues holding live performances all year. San Diego also has a plethora of theater and dance groups, including the La Jolla

Playhouse and the Moxie Theatre. San Diego is also home to the San Diego Symphony, which often plays in Copley Symphony Hall in Balboa Park.

San Diego offers a diverse range of exciting arts and culture events, from magnificent museums and galleries to bustling public art and music scenes. For those who like the arts, there is always something to enjoy.

Flowing waterfalls

Cedar Creek Falls

Three Sisters Falls

Eagle Creek Waterfall

Santa Ysabel Falls is number four

Palomar Mountain Waterfall

San Diego River Falls

Waterfall at San Elijo Lagoon

Waterfall at Mission Trails Regional Park

Iron Mountain Falls

Twin Falls, Idaho

Jungles to Explore

San Diego is a famous tourist and outdoor enthusiast destination, and one of the greatest ways to discover the region is to explore its rainforests. San Diego is home to numerous huge jungles and rainforests, each with its own distinct attractions and characteristics.

The San Diego Zoo Safari Park is one of the biggest and most popular jungles in the region. The park, located just north of the city, is home to nearly 3,000 species from all over the globe. Guests may get up up and personal with lions, elephants, giraffes, zebras, and other animals, as well as witness the unique and endangered California condor.

The Safari Park also has a number of interactive displays, such as the Tree house, a walk-through aviary, and a petting zoo.

The San Diego National Wildlife Refuge is located just east of downtown San Diego. This refuge is home to approximately 200 bird, animal, and reptile species, including the endangered California condor. The refuge also has various hiking routes that enable people to explore the region and watch animals in their natural environment.

Another fantastic jungle to visit in the San Diego region is the Cuyamaca Rancho State Park. The park, located east of the city, has approximately 40 miles of hiking trails and is home to a variety of local animals. Tourists may also enjoy the Old West beauty of neighboring Julian, which is noted for its apple orchards and old architecture.

The Anza-Borrego Desert State Park is situated east of San Diego and is one of the biggest state parks in the United States. The park is home to a diverse range of species, including coyotes, roadrunners, and bighorn sheep. The park also has various canyons, mountains, and washes, making it a perfect location for hiking, camping, and trekking.

San Diego is a terrific spot to explore rainforests, and these are just a few of the numerous alternatives.

San Diego is an excellent location for first-time tourists, thanks to its lush rainforests, diversified animals, and distinctive attractions.

So pack your luggage and be ready for an adventure!

Chapter 7

PRIMARY NEEDS IN SAN DIEGO

Accommodations options & prices

San Diego, with its stunning coastline, pleasant weather, and many activities, is an excellent first-time tourist location. San Diego's lodging options vary from low-cost hotels and motels to opulent resorts. Here is a rundown of some of the greatest alternatives in each price category.

Budgetary Considerations

There are many hotels and motels to select from if you want to stay on a tight budget. The Best Western Seven Seas is an excellent choice, with comfortable accommodations and facilities such as free Wi-Fi and an outdoor pool. A regular night's stay here costs between **$80 and $110** per person. The Days Inn San Diego Sea World is another excellent value choice, with rooms ranging from **$90 to $120** a night.

Budget Accommodations

Mid-range accommodations are ideal for individuals seeking a little extra comfort. The Handlery Hotel & Resort is an excellent option, with a wide range of hotel types, an outdoor pool and spa, and a restaurant. A room here is normally priced between **$130 and $200** per night.

The San Diego Marriott Gaslamp Quarter is another excellent choice, with accommodations ranging from **$180 to $250** per night.

Accommodations of the highest calibers

San Diego provides several possibilities for those seeking a genuinely premium vacation. The Omni San Diego Hotel, which has magnificent suites, a spa, and a pool with a private cabana area, is an excellent pick.

A room here is normally priced between **$250 and $400** per night. The Hard Rock Hotel San Diego is another excellent luxury alternative, with rooms ranging in price from **$275 to $450** per night.

San Diego has a wide range of excellent lodging alternatives to suit any budget. You'll be able to locate the appropriate spot to stay, from budget-friendly motels to opulent resorts.

Activities

1. Explore Balboa Park's museums, gardens, and attractions.

2. Explore the USS Midway Museum.

3. Take in the San Diego skyline while strolling along the bay.

4. Spend time at the beach, either surfing or sunbathing.

5. Take a stroll around the historic Gaslamp District.

6. Go on a San Diego Zoo guided tour.

7. Unwind with a craft beer at one of the numerous breweries.

8. Pay a visit to Coronado Island.

9. Visit Point Loma to go whale viewing.

10. Go on a food tour to enjoy the city's delectable cuisine.

Electric plugs

The electrical outlets in San Diego are the same as those found around the country. These are Type A and Type B outlets that take two or three prong plugs. In San Diego, the standard voltage is 120 volts.

Tour Packages

1. **San Diego City Tour**: Visit some of the city's most popular attractions, such as Balboa Park, Old Town, and the Gaslamp Quarter. Take a tour to learn about the city's history and culture.

2. **San Diego Zoo and Safari Park Tour:** Take a tour of two of the city's most popular attractions, the San Diego Zoo and the Safari

Park. Discover the secrets of the Zoo and Safari Park by getting up close and personal with exotic animals.

3. **SeaWorld San Diego Tour:** Enjoy the thrills and spills of SeaWorld San Diego. Explore the park, learn about marine life, and take in exciting rides and shows.

4. **Coronado Island Tour:** Take a guided tour of Coronado Island, a popular tourist destination off San Diego's coast. Visit the iconic Hotel del Coronado, go for a walk on the beach, and learn about the island's colorful history.

5. **La Jolla Tour:** Explore one of San Diego's most picturesque neighborhoods and its unique coastline and beaches.

Enjoy guided walking tours to discover La Jolla's hidden gems and natural beauty.

Chapter 8

DINING OUT & SHOPPING

Look no further than San Diego's diverse dining and shopping options for a one-of-a-kind and unforgettable experience. San Diego has something for everyone, from high-end restaurants to hole-in-the-wall markets and everything in between. You'll find something to your liking whether you're a foodie, a fashionista, or a shopaholic.

Dining out in San Diego will take you on a culinary journey that will tantalize your taste buds. From traditional Mexican dishes to trendy fusion fare, the city has more than enough options to satisfy even the most discriminating palate.

You'll find something to suit your needs, whether it's a romantic dinner on the beach or a quick bite on the go. Check out some of the city's well-known food trucks for a truly unique experience.

Shopping in San Diego is an adventure in and of itself. You're sure to find something to suit your style and budget among the abundance of boutique shops, large department stores, and everything in between.

San Diego has it all, whether you're looking for the latest trends or timeless classics. Furthermore, with its vibrant art scene, you'll have the opportunity to bring home a one-of-a-kind souvenir of your trip.

San Diego has it all, whether you're looking for a romantic dinner or a shopping spree. You're sure to have an unforgettable experience with its extensive dining and shopping options. Come explore the city and see what it has to offer.

Dining Out

San Diego is a vibrant city with a diverse range of dining options to suit every taste. There are some must-see attractions for first-time visitors.

Old Town Mexican Café is the place to go for traditional Mexican fare. This family-run restaurant serves traditional Mexican fare such as tacos, burritos, and enchiladas made from fresh, locally sourced ingredients.

If you're looking for something a little more upscale, go to Juniper & Ivy. Top Chef winner Richard Blais runs this innovative restaurant, which serves modern American dishes with unique twists.

Water Grill is a great option if you prefer seafood. Fresh, sustainably sourced seafood such as oysters, crab, and fish, as well as a variety of other dishes, can be found here.

San Diego's food scene is brimming with delicious options. Check out The Crack Shack for a truly one-of-a-kind experience. This hip restaurant serves fried chicken and egg dishes, as well as a full bar.

In San Diego, you're bound to find something delicious no matter what your mood is. Have a great time!

Places to Dine out

1. **The Lion's Share:** Located in San Diego's Gaslamp Quarter, this award-winning restaurant offers a fresh take on classic dishes made with locally sourced ingredients.

2. **The Crack Shack:** This restaurant serves globally inspired dishes such as adobo chicken sandwiches and jalapeno mac n' cheese.

3. **Ironside Fish & Oyster:** This seafood-focused restaurant serves a wide range of fresh seafood dishes as well as craft cocktails.

4. **The Patio on Goldfinch:** This restaurant serves a unique combination of Mediterranean and California-style dishes, as well as a selection of craft beers on tap.

5. **The Fish Market:** This well-known seafood restaurant serves a wide range of fresh seafood dishes as well as delectable sushi rolls.

6. **Prepkitchen Little Italy:** This Italian restaurant serves classic Italian dishes with a contemporary twist, as well as a selection of craft beers and wines.

Places to shop & what to Buy

As a first-time visitor, it can be difficult to decide what to buy in San Diego because there are so many great shopping options. Here are some of the best places to shop in San Diego, as well as some suggestions for what to buy.

1. **Seaport Village:** A great place to shop for souvenirs and trinkets to remember your trip to San Diego. Everything from t-shirts to art prints to jewelry is available.

2. **Fashion Valley Mall:** This mall is great for finding trendy items. Designer clothing from top brands such as Burberry, Michael Kors, and Gucci is available.

3. **Hillcrest Farmers Market:** The Hillcrest Farmers Market is a fantastic place to find locally grown produce, artisanal foods, and handmade crafts.

4. **Gaslamp Quarter:** The Gaslamp Quarter is a fantastic place to shop for trendy clothing, vintage finds, and one-of-a-kind gifts.

5. **Little Italy:** There are many unique boutiques and gift shops in Little Italy. Everything from jewelry to home decor to clothing is available.

6. **Balboa Park:** There are many unique stores and galleries in Balboa Park. Art prints, books, jewelry, and other items are available.

Whatever you're looking for, San Diego is sure to have something to make your trip memorable.

Antiquities Collection

The Ancient Egypt and Ancient Americas Galleries at the San Diego Museum of Man house a diverse collection of ancient artifacts from around the world. The museum's Ancient Egypt collection includes over 1,000 items, including mummies, statues, jewelry, and other cultural artifacts.

The Ancient Americas collection includes thousands of items from the Western Hemisphere's indigenous peoples, such as pottery, jewelry, and tools. In addition, the museum houses a collection of prehistoric artifacts from the San Diego area, such as stone tools and Native American basketry.

Ceramics Collection

The San Diego Museum of Art has a large and diverse ceramics collection that includes ancient world objects, Italian Renaissance maiolica, and contemporary studio pottery.

A large selection of Chinese ceramics from the Song, Yuan, Ming, and Qing Dynasties, as well as European and American pottery from the 18th and 19th centuries, are highlights of the collection.

Pieces from early Southwestern Native American cultures, such as the Hohokam and Mimbres, are also included in the collection.

In addition, the museum hosts a number of temporary and traveling exhibitions of ceramics from around the world.

Coptic Art Collection

Coptic art is on display at the San Diego Museum of Art in San Diego, California. Artifacts from Egypt and the Near East dating from the fourth to the seventh centuries are included in the collection. Textiles, pottery, jewelry, mosaics, and figurines are among the artifacts, many of which were used in religious ceremonies.

The works in the collection depict Coptic Christian culture, which thrived in the Mediterranean region between the fourth and seventh centuries. There is also a small collection of Coptic manuscripts and books at the museum. Religious texts, liturgical documents, and manuscripts from the early Coptic Church are among the works included in this collection.

Textiles Collection

The San Diego History Center houses a large textile collection containing clothing, textiles, and accessories dating from the nineteenth century to the present. Items from San Diego County, Southern California, and beyond are included in the collection.

Clothing, quilts, lace, flags, rugs, embroidery, and other textile-related items are among the items in the collection. The collection is especially strong in early twentieth-century clothing, with items from the Arts and Crafts Movement.

World War I, and World War II. A variety of items related to San Diego's military history are also included in the collection.

Chapter 9

HEALTH & SECURITY

San Diego's citizens and visitors alike place a premium on its health and safety. San Diego is one of the most popular cities in the United States, thanks to its beautiful beaches, world-renowned attractions, and diverse culture.

To ensure that its residents and visitors have a pleasant stay in San Diego, the city has taken proactive measures to ensure the health and safety of its citizens and visitors alike.

San Diego has a high standard of medical care and is served by a number of excellent healthcare providers. Medical facilities in the city range from community clinics and hospitals to specialized care centers and long-term care facilities.

San Diego also has highly trained professionals on call 24 hours a day, seven days a week to provide emergency medical care.

San Diego is also dedicated to providing a safe and secure environment for its residents and visitors. The city has an extensive emergency preparedness plan in place and is actively involved in disaster planning and response.

San Diego's police department is one of the most active and respected in the country, and the city has implemented a number of safety initiatives to help reduce crime and strengthen neighborhoods.

San Diego also has a number of programs and initiatives promoting healthy living and well-being. The city has invested in a variety of initiatives, such as bike-share programs, community gardens, and farmers markets, to improve access to healthy food and promote physical activity.

San Diego also has a number of projects and initiatives aimed at promoting mental health and well-being, including the San Diego Mental Health Initiative and the San Diego Regional Mental Health Services Program.

San Diego's health and safety are of the utmost importance, and the city is dedicated to providing a safe and secure environment for its residents and visitors.

San Diego is a vibrant and exciting city full of opportunity and adventure, and the city is committed to ensuring that its citizens and visitors have a safe and secure time in San Diego.

Health insurance

A variety of insurers offer health insurance in San Diego. Cigna, Aetna, Blue Cross Blue Shield, United Healthcare, Kaiser

Permanente, and Health Net are the most popular health insurance providers in San Diego.

Each of these companies offers a wide range of health insurance options and plans, so it is critical to compare them in order to find the best coverage for you. In addition, San Diego has a number of local and regional health insurance companies that can provide coverage.

Health Capacity

San Diego's health-care system has a large capacity. Over 250 hospitals, clinics, and health centers in the county offer a wide range of health services. Furthermore, San Diego has a large number of urgent care centers, retail clinics, and pharmacies to provide residents with quality care.

San Diego also has a high concentration of primary care physicians, mental health specialists, and specialists in fields ranging from oncology and orthopedics to cardiology and pediatrics.

San Diego has one of the highest concentrations of health care providers in the United States, with a population of over 3.3 million people.

Health-care facilities

*Sharp Memorial Hospital

*San Diego's Rady Children's Hospital

*Scripps Mercy Hospital

*UC San Diego Medical Center

*Palomar Medical Center

*Veterans Affairs San Diego Healthcare System

*Kaiser Permanente Medical Center in San Diego

*Alvarado Hospital Medical Center

*Sharp Grossmont Hospital

*Sharp Chula Vista Medical Center

Security Capacity

San Diego is well-known for its dedication to security and public safety. The city has taken a proactive approach to ensuring the safety of its residents and visitors. San Diego's security capacity is built on the city's proactive security approach.

San Diego has taken a number of precautions to ensure its security capacity. These safeguards include a variety of advanced technologies and procedures designed to protect the city and its residents.

San Diego monitors activity throughout the city with cutting-edge surveillance systems, advanced security cameras, and facial recognition technology. This aids in the prevention or detection of criminal activity.

San Diego also has a large network of emergency response teams, including the San Diego Police Department, Fire-Rescue Department, and Harbor Police. These teams are trained to respond quickly and efficiently in the event of an emergency.

San Diego also employs a number of sophisticated security systems. These systems are intended to detect and respond to any security threats that may exist in the area.

San Diego has implemented an integrated vehicle registration system that allows law enforcement to identify vehicles and their owners quickly. San Diego has also implemented a citywide public safety alert system to quickly notify residents and visitors of any hazards in the area.

Furthermore, San Diego has an active Neighborhood Watch program through which residents and visitors can report suspicious activity. The program is intended to foster community and collaboration between residents and law enforcement.

San Diego also has a robust security infrastructure in the form of private security firms. These businesses have been trained to recognize and respond to security threats in the area. They also offer a number of services such as alarm monitoring, home security systems, and personal protection.

Overall, San Diego has taken a proactive approach to public safety and security. To ensure its security capacity, the city has implemented a variety of measures, including advanced technologies, extensive emergency response teams, sophisticated security systems, and private security companies.

These measures have contributed to San Diego being one of the safest cities in the country.

Security services

Security services are critical in San Diego, which has a population of almost 1.4 million people. San Diegans depend on security services to secure their property and keep them safe, from personal residences to businesses and government facilities.

San Diego security services vary from simple monitoring to complex security systems. Basic security services may comprise surveillance cameras and motion detectors that notify a monitoring service when motion is detected. Depending on the requirements of the client, these services may be monitored remotely or locally.

Access control, video surveillance, and alarm systems are examples of advanced security systems. Access control systems may be used to restrict who is allowed to enter and depart a company or building, whilst video surveillance systems allow for remote monitoring of a facility. Unauthorized access, smoke or fire, and other security hazards may all be detected by alarm systems.

Security guards are another choice for companies and households in San Diego. Security guards are educated and accredited by the state of California and may provide security beyond surveillance cameras and alarm systems. Hired security guards may patrol a site or offer a visible presence to dissuade unwanted entrance.

San Diego security services may involve investigative services. Private investigators may be engaged to look into suspicious behavior, theft, or other types of criminal conduct. Private investigators may also do background checks, locate missing people, and offer surveillance services.

Whichever sort of security services you want in San Diego, there is almost certainly a business that can supply them. Security businesses in San Diego can assist you whether you want simple monitoring or complex security systems, security guards, or investigative services.

It is important to do research and discover a firm that provides high-quality services at a fair cost.

Chapter 10

SURVIVAL GUIDE

What you Get when following survival Guide as a first time visitor to San Diego

* **Acquire critical skills:** Following a survival guide may teach you critical skills that can help you remain alive in a dangerous circumstance. You may learn how to make a shelter, collect food and water, and use a compass and map to navigate.

* **Conserve money :** By learning how to adapt with what you currently have by following a survival guide. You may, for example, learn how to start a fire without matches or how to filter water without a filter.

* **Increase your confidence:** Knowing you can live in the woods with little resources will give you the courage to explore more and go on more adventures. Developing survival skills may also aid in the development of problem-solving abilities and ingenuity.

* Have fun in the outdoors: Using a survival guide may help you make the most of your time outside. You may learn to recognize food plants and fauna, as well as how to care for yourself while camping. This has the potential to open up a whole new universe of outdoor activities.

Tips learn San Diego language

Begin with the Fundamentals: If you're a first-time visitor to San Diego, the best method to learn the language is to begin with the fundamentals.

Learn simple Spanish words and expressions such as "hola" (hello), "gracias" (thank you), "por favor" (please), and "adiós" (goodbye). Understanding these words will make you feel immediately more at ease while conversing with San Diegans.

Practice with Native Speakers: Practice your Spanish with native speakers if feasible. There is a flourishing Hispanic population in San Diego, and there are several chances to learn the language. Try taking a class, joining a discussion group, or just conversing with the locals.

Listen and Repeat: An good technique to learn the language is to listen to fluent Spanish speakers and repeat what they say. Listen to Spanish-language radio or podcasts and practice repeating the words and phrases you hear.

Understand Regional Variations: Since Spanish is spoken differently in various places, it's crucial to study the dialects spoken in San Diego. The letter "ll," for example, is often pronounced as a "y" in San Diego Spanish.

Employ Technology: Technology may be an excellent tool for learning a language. There are several online classes, apps, and websites that may assist you in learning the fundamentals of Spanish. Several are free or low-cost, allowing you to get started right away.

Watch Spanish-Language TV: Another excellent technique to learn the language is to watch Spanish-language television. You will not only be able to detect distinct accents and dialects, but you will also have a greater knowledge of the context in which words and phrases are employed.

Immerse Yourself: Immersing oneself in a language is one of the finest methods to learn it. Spend time in Spanish-speaking regions and learn the language with natives. Even if you don't comprehend everything right away, you'll eventually have a greater understanding.

Learning the language of San Diego is an excellent approach to make the most of your trip. You'll be speaking the language like a native in no time with a little effort and practice.

Tips to learn San Diego culture

San Diego has a strong cultural past and provides many first-time tourists a variety of experiences. Here are some pointers to help you learn about the culture of San Diego and make the most of your vacation.

Explore the local attractions: Spend some time visiting San Diego's various attractions. There's something for everyone in San Diego, from the world-famous San Diego Zoo to the quirky Gaslamp Quarter and Balboa Park. Explore the museums, enjoy a harbor boat, or relax on the beach.

Dine locally: San Diego has one of the most active culinary scenes in the country. Local fish tacos, burritos, and Mexican meals are recommended. Check out the craft beer scene as well. San Diego is home to some of the country's top craft brewers.

Take in the culture: San Diego has a thriving arts and music scene. Spend some time touring the galleries, going to concerts, and seeing plays. Spend some time exploring the distinct neighborhoods and street art.

Get active: San Diego is a fantastic city for becoming involved in the community. Participate in a community service project, a public meeting, or a neighborhood festival. This is a fantastic opportunity to meet new people and learn about the area.

Speak to the locals: The greatest approach to learn about San Diego culture is to talk to the people. Inquire about the history of the city, the finest places to dine, and their favorite pastimes. You'll receive an insider's viewpoint as well as some fantastic advice.

Following these suggestions will assist you in becoming acquainted with San Diego and its culture.

Spend some time touring the city and getting to know the people that live there. You will undoubtedly have a memorable time.

Tips to avoid scammers

San Diego is a popular vacation location for many travelers, with several sights and activities. Sadly, it may also be a location where frauds thrive, so visitors should take steps to avoid being taken advantage of. Here are some suggestions to assist you avoid scams when in San Diego:

•**Do Your Research:** Before you go, learn about the city and the locations you want to visit. This study might assist you in being aware of possible scams and frauds in the region.

•**Be Alert:** Keep an eye out for any suspicious behavior or persons. Be extra careful around tourist sites and regions, since they are popular targets for fraudsters.

•**Employ Common Sense:** Don't believe strangers who offer too-good-to-be-true offers, and never give out sensitive information to strangers. Be careful of anybody who demands payment in advance for services or products.

•**Use Reputable Stores** and Businesses: While shopping in San Diego, choose reputed shops and companies. Avoid purchasing things from strangers or street sellers since they may be counterfeit or stolen.

•**Utilize Credit Cards:** While making purchases, use a credit card wherever feasible. Credit cards provide more security than cash and allow you to contest fraudulent payments.

•**Know Your Rights**: Be sure you understand your consumer rights and what safeguards you have if you are a victim of a scam.

•**Report Scams:** If you believe you have been a victim of a fraud, contact the authorities right once.

You may help prevent yourself from being a victim of a scam in San Diego by following these easy guidelines.

Take the time to explore your surroundings and be aware of your surroundings, and always use common sense and prudence.

GUIDES

1. **Understand the Climate:** San Diego is renowned for its warm and sunny weather, so knowing what to anticipate while visiting the city is essential. The typical temperature in San Diego is between 65 and 75 degrees Fahrenheit, so pack appropriately. The city also receives a lot of sunlight, so carry lots of sunscreen and sunglasses.

2. **Visit the Neighborhoods:** San Diego is divided into various communities, each with its own distinct culture and attractions. Spend some time exploring the various areas to gain a better sense of the city and identify the finest spots to visit.

3. **Understand Your Public Transportation Options:** San Diego has an extensive public transit system that includes buses, light rail, trolleys, and other modes of transportation. Make an effort to get acquainted with the various modes of transportation available so that you can navigate the city more simply.

4. **See the Beaches:** San Diego is home to some of the world's most gorgeous beaches. Spend some time exploring the beaches and admiring the breathtaking scenery.

5. **Take Use of Outdoor Activities:** San Diego has an abundance of outdoor activities, ranging from hiking to surfing. Take advantage of the city's outdoor activities, since they are a terrific opportunity to see the city while also getting some exercise.

6. **Visit the Tourism Attractions:** From the world-famous San Diego Zoo to the USS Midway Museum, San Diego has a wide range of tourist attractions. Visit these sights while in San Diego to enjoy the whole San Diego experience.

7. **Enjoy the Nightlife:** San Diego has a thriving evening culture, with several bars, clubs, and restaurants to pick from. Check out some of the city's top locations and enjoy the nightlife.

8. **Taste the Local Cuisine:** San Diego is famed for its incredible cuisine, so make time to try some of the local fare. In San Diego, there is something for everyone, from Mexican to seafood.

9. **Locate Accommodations:** From hotels to vacation rentals, San Diego provides a broad range of options. Be certain to choose the greatest selection for your budget and requirements.

10. **Have Fun**: Above all, remember to have fun on your vacation!

San Diego offers something for everyone, so take your time exploring the city and have a good time.

Get used to public transportation

Learning to utilize public transit while on vacation in San Diego may be a terrific way to save money and travel about the city without needing to hire a vehicle.

San Diego's public transportation system is quite broad and simple to use, so even if you are new with public transit, you will have no trouble getting about the city. Here are some pointers to help you adjust to public transportation during your San Diego trip.

• **Investigate San Diego's Public Transportation System:** Spend some time researching and becoming acquainted with San Diego's public transit system. In San Diego, there are numerous modes of public transit available, including buses, trolleybuses, and the San Diego Trolley. Plan your excursions ahead of time by researching routes and timings.

• **Get a Transport Pass:** If you want to utilize public transportation regularly during your trip, purchase a transit pass. If you intend to utilize public transportation more than a few times, San Diego offers many kinds of transit passes that may save you money.

• **Get Assistance:** Don't be hesitant to seek assistance if you need it. Staff at transit hubs and on buses are very pleasant and eager to assist you if you have any concerns or want instructions.

• **Provide Enough of Time:** Let yourself plenty of time to get at your location. Public transit may be unreliable at times, and there may be delays. It is usually preferable to be early than than late, so prepare appropriately.

• **Be Conscious of Your Surroundings:** While riding public transit, be alert of your surroundings. Keep a watch on your valuables and be on the lookout for strange persons or actions.

You can become adjusted to public transportation during your San Diego trip by following these guidelines. Without the inconvenience of renting a vehicle, public transit may be a terrific way to explore the city.

Just remember to conduct your homework, get a transportation ticket if required, and always be alert of your surroundings.

Chapter 11

HIDDEN GEMS TO DISCOVER

La Jolla Cove

La Jolla Cove is a breathtakingly beautiful beach in San Diego, California. It is located in the La Jolla neighborhood, which is well-known for its scenic views, upscale shopping, and world-class restaurants.

The Cove is famous for its crystal clear waters and dramatic cliffs on the Pacific Ocean. Because the visibility is among the best in the area, The Cove is a popular spot for swimming, snorkeling, and scuba diving.

The Cove is also a haven for sea life, including sea lions, seals, leopard sharks, and the occasional dolphin. It's also a great place to go whale watching.

> **La Jolla Cove is a popular destination for both tourists and locals, and it is easily accessible by car or bicycle.**

Cabrillo National Monument

Cabrillo National Monument is a National Monument of the United States located in San Diego, California. The monument, which is located at the southern tip of the Point Loma Peninsula, commemorates Juan Rodriguez Cabrillo's landing in San Diego Bay on September 28, 1542.

This was the first time a European explorer set foot on what is now the United States' West Coast, and it marked the beginning of European exploration of the Pacific Coast.

The visitor center at the monument includes exhibits about Cabrillo and San Diego history, as well as a film about the historic landing. The grounds of the monument include a museum, old lighthouses, and a short trail leading to the actual landing site.

Guided tours of the monument, including a walk around the Bayside Trail, are available from park rangers. The monument also serves as a sanctuary for a variety of plants and animals, including the endangered San Diego subspecies of the California least tern.

Cabrillo National Monument is open all year, with varying hours depending on the season.

Except for **Thanksgiving and Christmas Day, the monument is open from 9:00 a.m. to 5:00 p.m. daily. Everyone is welcome to visit the monument.**

Mission Trails Regional Park

Mission Trails Regional Park, located in San Diego, California, is a 7,220 acre natural park. It is one of the largest urban parks in the United States and provides visitors with a variety of outdoor activities.

There are over 60 miles of hiking, biking, and equestrian trails in the park, as well as many parks, picnic areas, and campgrounds. It also has two lakes, Kumeyaay Lake and San Vicente Reservoir, which offer a variety of water activities like fishing, kayaking, and canoeing.

The park is home to a diverse range of wildlife, including birds, reptiles, and mammals, all of which can be seen in the nearby Kumeyaay Lake Ecological Reserve.

The park also provides educational programs and volunteer opportunities, making it an excellent location for getting involved in the local community.

Torrey Pines State Natural Reserve

Torrey Pines State Natural Reserve is a well-known 2,000-acre park located on San Diego's Pacific coast. The Torrey Pine tree, which grows only in this area, is found in the reserve.

The reserve is also well-known for its miles of spectacular coastal trails, which offer visitors breathtaking views of the Pacific Ocean and the surrounding landscape.

The reserve is free to enter and open all year, with hours varying depending on the season. Hikers, nature lovers, and beachgoers all flock to this popular destination.

The reserve's trails range in difficulty from easy to moderate, making it suitable for people of all abilities. Visitors can see a variety of plants, wildflowers, and wildlife along the trails, including jackrabbits, coyotes, bobcats, and even the occasional mountain lion.

Torrey Pines State Natural Reserve has a number of unique attractions in addition to the trails. The Guy Fleming Trail, an interpretive boardwalk trail that winds through the reserve's unique ecosystem; the Torrey Pines Gliderport, which offers hang gliding and paragliding lessons; and the Torrey Pines State Beach, a pristine sandy beach popular for swimming, surfing, and other beach activities, are just a few examples.

The reserve is also well-known for its educational programs and special events. Visitors can learn about the reserve's history, ecology, and geology through ranger-led programs, and there are also special events such as bird walks, full moon hikes, and interpretive talks. Torrey Pines State Natural Reserve also offers a number of volunteer opportunities for visitors to assist in the care and protection of the reserve's unique resources.

Torrey Pines State Natural Reserve has something for everyone, whether you're looking for a peaceful nature escape, a fun day at the beach, or an educational experience.

> **It's no surprise that the reserve has become one of San Diego's most beloved destinations, with its stunning landscape, diverse attractions, and educational opportunities.**

Sunset Cliffs Natural Park

Sunset Cliffs Natural Park, located in San Diego, California, is a 68-acre park. The park is located on a rugged stretch of southern California coastline with dramatic cliffs, rocky shorelines, and breathtaking ocean views.

The park has a number of trails and pathways that allow visitors to explore the area and enjoy the breathtaking views from a variety of vantage points.

The Sunset Cliffs Trail, which provides access to the park's eastern edge, the Coastal Trail, which winds along the coast, and the Point Loma Trail, which provides views of the San Diego skyline, are the most popular trails.

The park also contains several beaches, including Sunset Cliffs Beach, Luscomb's Point Beach, and Point Loma Beach. Swimming, surfing, and fishing are just a few of the activities available at these beaches.

The park also has a diverse wildlife population, including sea lions, dolphins, and seabirds. The park is also a popular destination for whale watching, as gray whales migrate along the coast each winter and spring.

Sunset Cliffs Natural Park is a popular destination for visitors who want to take in the breathtaking views, explore the wildlife, and appreciate the natural beauty of the California coast.

Balboa Park

San Diego's Balboa Park is one of the city's most beautiful and iconic attractions. This 1,200-acre park in the heart of downtown San Diego is home to some of the city's most beloved attractions, including the world-famous San Diego Zoo, various museums, lush gardens, and stunning Spanish Colonial Revival architecture. Balboa Park is the ideal place to spend a day in the city, with over 15,000 trees, gardens, and attractions.

The San Diego Zoo is one of Balboa Park's most popular attractions. This world-famous zoo is the largest in the United States and is home to some of the world's most exotic species.

The zoo offers a variety of experiences for all ages, from the popular Panda experience to the interactive Discovery Outpost. Aside from the zoo, Balboa Park is also home to the San Diego Air & Space Museum and the Timken Museum of Art.

Balboa Park's botanical gardens are some of the most beautiful in the city. There is something for everyone, from the breathtaking Hibiscus Garden to the tranquil Japanese Friendship Garden. In addition, Balboa Park is home to some of San Diego's most beautiful architecture. This park is a must-see for all visitors due to its Spanish-style buildings, courtyards, and plazas.

Throughout the year, Balboa Park hosts a variety of events. The park is a great place to experience some of San Diego's culture, from the annual December Nights celebration to the summer concert series. In addition, there are tennis courts, hiking trails, a golf course, and a skate park for visitors to enjoy.

Balboa Park is the ideal location for visitors to discover and enjoy San Diego. This park is one of the most beautiful and iconic locations in the city, thanks to its spectacular gardens.

World-famous attractions, and stunning architecture. Balboa Park is the ideal location for a day of adventure or peaceful relaxation.

Old Town San Diego State Historic Park

The Old Town San Diego State Historic Park is a state park in San Diego, California's Old Town neighborhood. The park preserves and recreates the early days of San Diego, which was the first European settlement on what is now the United States' western coast.

The park features historical structures, a plaza, gardens, a museum, and other attractions. The park is free to enter and open daily from 9 a.m. to 5 p.m. For a fee, guided tours that include a visit to the museum are available. The park is home to some of San Diego's oldest structures, including the Casa de Estudillo, Mason Street School, Robinson-Rose House, San Diego Union Printing Office, and Whaley House.

Throughout the year, the park hosts a variety of events and festivals.

Coronado Beach

Coronado Beach in San Diego is one of the world's most beautiful beaches. It's a great place to spend a relaxing day or to take in some of the amazing views the area has to offer, and it's located just south of the city center.

The beach stretches the entire length of Coronado Island and offers a wide sandy shoreline as well as a variety of activities. There are numerous swimming areas, including a designated swimming area and lifeguard-protected areas. Water sports enthusiasts will find plenty to do, including swimming, surfing, kayaking, and stand-up paddle boarding.

Coronado Beach is also a popular destination for families. The beach has a playground, a picnic area, and a variety of beach activities. Visitors can also walk along the boardwalk, visit some of the unique shops and restaurants, or rent a beach cruiser to explore the island.

The famous Hotel Del Coronado and its beachfront courtyard, the Coronado Ferry Landing, which offers great views of the San Diego skyline, and the Coronado Municipal Golf Course are also located in the area.

Coronado Beach is sure to impress no matter what time of year you visit.

> **With its breathtaking views, warm waters, and plethora of activities, it's no surprise that millions of people visit this iconic beach each year.**

The Gaslamp Quarter

The Gaslamp Quarter is a 16-block National Historic District in downtown San Diego that is filled with Victorian-style buildings and has a vibrant nightlife, shopping, dining, and entertainment scene. The Gaslamp Quarter, located near the San Diego Bay waterfront, is a popular destination for both locals and visitors.

The Gaslamp Quarter, formerly known as "New Town," was founded in the late 1800s and is one of San Diego's oldest neighborhoods. The transformation of the area from a seedy neighborhood to a vibrant entertainment and shopping district began in the 1970s, when restoration efforts were launched to bring the area back to life.

Today, the Gaslamp Quarter is a popular tourist and local destination, with a variety of attractions, entertainment, and restaurants. The neighborhood is home to an eclectic mix of restaurants and bars serving cuisine from all over the world. There are upscale dining establishments as well as casual eateries, as well as a number of nightclubs and live music venues.

The Gaslamp Quarter also has a diverse range of shops, from high-end boutiques to vintage and thrift stores. Clothing and souvenirs, as well as books and antiques, are available to visitors. There are also several art galleries and museums, as well as historical buildings and sites.

Throughout the year, the Gaslamp Quarter hosts a variety of events, from the annual Mardi Gras celebration to the San Diego Comic-Con International. The area also hosts a number of festivals, such as the San Diego International Film Festival, December Nights in Balboa Park, and the San Diego Pride Parade.

Whatever your interests are, the Gaslamp Quarter has something for you.

The Gaslamp Quarter has something for everyone, whether you're looking for a fun night out or a one-of-a-kind shopping experience.

San Diego Zoo

San Diego Zoo is a world-renowned wildlife sanctuary in San Diego's Balboa Park. The San Diego Zoo, founded in 1916, is home to over 3,700 animals from 650 species, making it one of the world's largest zoos.

As one of San Diego's most popular tourist attractions, the zoo provides a variety of activities and attractions for visitors of all ages.

The Safari Park, a sprawling 1,800-acre wildlife preserve where visitors can get up close and personal with elephants, giraffes, and cheetahs, is one of the San Diego Zoo's most popular attractions.

The Safari Park also has a variety of habitats, such as African Plains, Asian Savanna, and Gorilla Forest, where visitors can see many different species in their natural habitats.

The San Diego Zoo has a number of educational programs and exhibits for those interested in learning more about conservation.

The zoo's Global Reach program contributes to global conservation efforts, and its Conservation Research Centers have conducted research on a wide range of species and habitats, from sea turtles to chimps. There are also interactive exhibits at the zoo, such as the Reptile House, where visitors can learn about reptile habitats, life cycles, and behaviors.

Throughout the year, the San Diego Zoo also hosts a number of special events and activities, such as the Nighttime Zoo, a summer-long evening series that includes live music and performances, as well as behind-the-scenes tours and animal encounters.

The zoo also offers guided tours, such as the Behind the Scenes Tour and the Penguin Encounter Tour, for those who want to get a closer look at the animals.

The San Diego Zoo has something for everyone, regardless of age or interest.

The San Diego Zoo, with its diverse collection of animals, habitats, and activities, is a must-see for any first-time visitor to San Diego.

Chapter 12

FREE MAP APPS FOR LOCATIONS

Whether you're in town for business or pleasure, a map app can be a lifeline for your travels. San Diego is a large and diverse city, making getting around difficult. You can easily get directions to any destination, find points of interest and local attractions, and explore the city without getting lost using a map app.

Map apps provide an accurate and up-to-date view of the city and can assist you in avoiding traffic and other stumbling blocks. You can easily find the best route to your destination and get an estimated time of arrival. You can also use a map app to find nearby restaurants, bars, and shops, ensuring that you never miss out on the best places to visit in the city.

Map apps are also useful for finding public transportation routes, so you don't get lost or miss your stop. You can also easily find parking spots, which is extremely useful when trying to get around town.

Map apps can also provide weather and event information, allowing you to plan your activities accordingly. You can also receive notifications about new attractions and activities, ensuring that you don't miss out. Finally, map apps can be a great way to learn about new places and activities that you might not have known about otherwise.

A map app can be a great tool for exploring San Diego, whether you're here for a short visit or an extended stay. With the right app, you can easily navigate the city and avoid missing out on any of the unique experiences that this amazing city has to offer.

Location Map Apps for Free

1. **San Diego City Guide:** This app offers a comprehensive reference to the city of San Diego, including maps, attractions, restaurants, and other information. It also includes a map, which enables you to explore the city and find your way about.

2. **San Diego Tour Guide:** This free app gives a thorough tour to the city, including detailed maps, attractions, and other information. It also includes information about local events and activities.

3. **San Diego Offline Maps & Navigation:** This free program gives a thorough map of San Diego, making it simple to navigate the city. It also has a searchable database of attractions, restaurants, and other businesses.

4. **San Diego Travel Guide:** This free app gives a comprehensive picture of San Diego, including detailed maps, attractions, and other information. It also has an interactive map to help you plan your journey.

How to Use a Free Map App

While traveling, using a free map app to assist you make your way around a new city or unfamiliar location may be a useful tool. Whether you're searching for the next coffee shop or planning a cross-country road trip, having a trustworthy map app may be quite useful. Here's an explanation on how to utilize a free map app.

Step 1. **Install the app:** The first step is to install the map app on your smartphone. The majority of popular map applications are free on both iOS and Android smartphones. Browse your device's app store for the map app you wish to use and download it.

Step 2. **Determine your location:** After installing the app, launch it and provide it access to your location. This enables the app to locate your precise position on the map.

Step 3. **Look for a place to stay**: After your position has been determined, utilize the search field to choose a destination. You may look for an address, a company name, or even a category of business (like coffee shop). The app will then display you your destination's location.

Step 4. **Get instructions:** You may acquire instructions to your location after you've recognized it. The app will offer you the optimal route to take as well as turn-by-turn instructions.

Step 5. **See the map:** You may also display a map of the area you are now in. This will show you the local streets, shops, parks, and other sights. This might be useful if you're looking for a certain street or company.

Step 6. **Distribute the map:** Several map applications also let you share the map with your friends and family. This might come in handy if you're planning a vacation together or need to show someone where you are.

Using a free map app to explore a new city or unfamiliar location may be a terrific way to learn more about it.

You can simply navigate your way around and get at your destination fast and securely with the correct software.

List of map in San Diego

*Map of San Diego County
    *Street Map of San Diego
    *Map of the San Diego Freeways

*Tourism Map of San Diego

*San Diego Bicycle Map

*Map of San Diego Beaches

*Topographic Map of San Diego

*Map of San Diego Zip Codes

*Map of San Diego Hiking

*Map of San Diego

Neighborhoods

Chapter 13

SOLO TRIP & MEAL PLAN

San Diego! Such a wonderful moment for you to be here. This lovely city has a plethora of activities, sights, and natural treasures to discover. Whether you go alone or in a group, it will undoubtedly be a wonderful experience.

One of the first things you should think about while planning a solo vacation is your lunch plan. There are several restaurants, cafés, and food trucks to select from in San Diego. Here are some suggestions for selecting the best meal plan for your vacation to ensure you get the most out of your stay.

Determine your budget: San Diego has a wide range of eating alternatives, from quick-service eateries to sophisticated, gourmet restaurants. You should choose a meal package that meets your budget and enables you to enjoy your vacation without going broke.

Pick what kind of meal you want: San Diego is well-known for its seafood and Mexican cuisine, but there are many more possibilities. Decide what sort of cuisine you want to eat and look at the menus of nearby restaurants.

Create a food plan: Knowing what you're going to eat each day can help you remain on track and ensure you don't miss out on any of San Diego's excellent cuisine. Include snacks and beverages in your meal plan as well.

Don't forget about the city's many meal delivery options: There are many delivery businesses in San Diego that will bring your meals directly to your door. This is a terrific way to save time and money, and you'll be able to enjoy your lunch without ever leaving your hotel room.

With a little forethought, you can make your single vacation to San Diego as delectable and pleasurable as possible. Best wishes!

A week Solo journey for first time visitor

Day 1: Begin your day by strolling around Balboa Park, one of San Diego's major urban parks. See the gardens, museums, and Spanish-style architecture. Next, ride the famous Balboa Park Carousel for a leisurely spin.

Day 2: Spend the morning touring Old Town San Diego, California's birthplace. See its numerous historical attractions and stroll through its gorgeous plazas and cobblestone lanes. Afterwards, relax with a leisurely lunch at one of the city's wonderful restaurants.

Day 3: Enjoy a day at the beach! Some of the nicest beaches in the world may be found in San Diego. Pick from the various family-friendly beaches along the coast or a more private one.

Day 4: Discover San Diego's thriving arts and entertainment scene. Take in a performance at one of its numerous performing arts venues or peruse the works of local artists at one of its many galleries.

Day 5: Spend the day visiting the San Diego Zoo, one of the biggest and most well-known zoos in the world. Take a walk around its gorgeous grounds and meet the exotic animals.

Day 6: Visit the adjacent city of La Jolla for the day. Discover its beautiful beaches, lovely boutiques, and delectable eateries.

Day 7: Finish your journey by checking out San Diego's vibrant nightlife. Pick from its many pubs and clubs, or see a concert at one of its several live music venues.

A week meal plan for first timer in San Diego

Sunday: Begin your week in San Diego with a traditional fish taco from one of the city's numerous taco stands.

Monday: Dine at some of the city's greatest eateries in the Gaslamp District.

Tuesday: Enjoy the city's lovely outdoor areas by having a picnic at Balboa Park.

Wednesday: Spend the evening in Little Italy sampling the delectable Italian food.

Thursday: Have some Mexican cuisine in Old Town San Diego.

Friday: Visit the Fish Market for some of the tastiest seafood in town.

Saturday: Take a cuisine tour around San Diego's North Park area to learn about the unique tastes.

Conclusion

San Diego is a lovely and dynamic city on California's Pacific coast. It is well-known for its beautiful beaches, pleasant weather, world-class attractions, and delectable cuisine. Surfing, boating, bicycling, and seeing the city's various attractions are just a few of the activities available to visitors to San Diego.

San Diego also has a number of cultural attractions, such as the world-renowned San Diego Zoo, SeaWorld, and the notorious Balboa Park. There are also a variety of distinct neighborhoods to discover, each with its own distinct personality and charm.

San Diego is an excellent choice for individuals seeking a distinctive and thrilling vacation experience. San Diego offers something for everyone, whether you're searching for a calm beach vacation or an action-packed adventure. San Diego is the ideal location for tourists of all ages and interests, thanks to its beautiful beaches, various activities, and pleasant weather.

Thus, if you're seeking for the ideal holiday spot, San Diego is the place to go. San Diego, with its laid-back vibe and limitless diversions, is the ideal destination to unwind and unwind.

So, what are you holding out for? Come see all San Diego has to offer and prepare for the vacation of a lifetime!

Printed in Great Britain
by Amazon